Focus on China Series

China's Population Situation and Policies

Wu Cangping & Mu Guangzong

Foreign Languages Press

First Edition 2004

Translated by: Zhang Tingquan
English text edited by: Paul White & Huang Youyi

Home Page:
http://www.flp.com.cn
E-mail Addresses:
info@flp.com.cn
sales@flp.com.cn

ISBN 7-119-03326-3
© Foreign Languages Press, Beijing, China, 2004
Published by Foreign Languages Press
24 Baiwanzhuang Road, Beijing 100037, China
Distributed by China International Book Trading Corporation
35 Chegongzhuang Xilu, Beijing 100044, China
P.O. Box 399, Beijing, China
Printed in the People's Republic of China

Contents

Preface

Population is an important and chronic variable that affects a country's development. The Chinese population problem, generally speaking, has two aspects: One, the problem of population control, that is, how to alleviate the pressure of the consumption demand arising from population growth by controlling the growth of the population; and two, the problem of how to change the population burden into a benefit through human capital investment and the development of human resources.

So far as population control is concerned, "the development of man" will bring about a fundamental change in the birth policy of the individual persons and families — from the birth policy of the family standard deeply affected by the traditional culture to the personal standard birth policy which can better manifest the rationality of the market economy, namely, from early marriage, early birth, partiality for male babies, more births and more babies to late marriage, late birth, fewer births and healthy babies, thus turning the conflict into harmony between the micro birth policy and macro control goal. "The development of man" dealt with here is embodied mainly in the improvement of the educational level and the rise of the social and economic status of the general population. Many studies have shown that the employment of better-educated women of childbearing age in the non-agricultural fields is very helpful for the achievement of a low birth rate. In fact, the visible drop of the birth rate in China in the past twenty years is inseparable from the improvement of the education and employment of Chinese women. In short, the modernization of man will bring about a revolutionary change in the birth policy of the Chinese people. The drop in the urban birth rate is an indication of this. Fewer but healthier children who are provided with the best possible care and education is now the standard ambition of the majority of urban people. In the countryside, the problem of population control will be increasingly linked to the blending of town and country.

China has a surplus of raw human resources, but a deficiency of special human resources, namely educated and skilled people. The problem of the low educational level of the majority of the population has existed for a long time. Only by placing emphasis on the strategy of the "development of man", can China really bring up a high-quality labor force that can compete in the international community and meet the needs of the development of the market economy, thereby laying a firm foundation in terms of human capital and human resources for the sustainable development of China.

To adopt the "development of man" as the strategy for sustainable development is a reliable choice for coming out of the dilemma of the increase of low-quality population. The population issue is not simply a question of population increase and control. To be sure population control is a necessary condition for realizing development goals, the most important question, however, is to invest in and develop the existing population. In short, the investment in man is the most important investment and the development of man is the most important development. To realize this and do so will surely allow China, the most populous country in the world, to write a glorious chapter in the 21st century.

Chapter 1

A Huge Population Is China's Most Basic and Characteristic National Condition

It is universally acknowledged that there are too many people in China, and therefore the population must be controlled by means of family planning.

At present, the population on the Chinese mainland has reached 1,265,830,000. If the Chinese people in the Hong Kong, Macao and Taiwan regions are also accounted, the total Chinese population comes to 1,295,330,000. This means that China is the most populous country in the world, having more people than the total of all the populations in the developed countries and regions.

The solutions to many problems in China, major or minor, are all related to the basic factor of its large population.

(1) Why Is It Said That the Chinese Population Is Too Large?

The huge population has always been a basic national condition in contemporary and modern China. The "problem of too many people"[1] [1]emerged over a century ago. The Chinese population exceeded 100 million in the middle of the

---

[1] This problem is central to Gong Zizhen's "Immigration Theory," Wang Shiduo's "Birth Control Theory" Tan Sitong's "Overpopulation Theory" and Yan Fu's "Evolution Theory."

17th century, and rose to 300 or 400 million 200 years later. After the mid-18th century, the problem of "more people and less farmland" became more and more acute, developing into a focus of social contradictions. The excessive and rapid growth of the Chinese population began to arouse more and more concern and discussion.[2] Overpopulation had become a national problem by the 19th century. The contradiction between population growth and the shortage of land resources further aggravated the class contradictions under the historical conditions of the time, and became a major cause of social crisis and upheavals. Luo Ergang, He Bingdi and other historians held the view that behind the outbreak of the Taiping (Heavenly Peace) Revolution (1851-1864) was the pressure of population growth, a historical factor that cannot be neglected. Karl Max suggested, one year before the Taiping Revolution, that the slow but growing overpopulation in China had already turned its social conditions into heavy shackles for the majority of its people.[3]

However, the fastest population growth was witnessed after the founding of the People's Republic of China — from 540 million in the early years of the People's Republic to double that figure in the following 40 years, with an average increase of 100 million every seven years. In mid-February 1995, it surpassed the 1.2 billion mark. The fifth national census conducted in 2000 showed that China's population was close to 1.3 billion.

Overpopulation has posed tremendous challenges to the economic construction in China. Confronted by the world's largest population, China has a very limited living environment. If the country does not make big efforts to control its population, the "trouble of having too many people" will undoubtedly become even more serious in the future and the

4

ability of the environment to accommodate such a population will come to a breaking point.

The areas of habitable plains and rolling country in China account for 12 percent and 9.9 percent of the total land area, respectively. Basins, mountains and plateaus account for 18.8 percent, 33.3 percent and 26 percent, respectively, of China's territory. Most of the basins, which are mainly inhospitable deserts, are located in northwest China, such as the Qaidam, Junggar and Tarim basins. There are even more areas on the mountains and plateaus that are not suitable for living. From another angle, the humid and semi-humid areas in China that are suitable for habitation account for 32 percent and 15 percent, respectively, while the dry and semi-dry areas account for 31 percent and 22 percent, respectively. On the basis of the figures collected during the third census in 1982, the National Bureau of Statistics estimated that 20.3 percent of the Chinese population lived in areas with poor living conditions at or higher than 500 meters above sea level, and half of them lived at or higher than 1,000 meters above sea level. Only an average of 10 percent of the world's people live at or higher than 400 meters above sea level.

Professor Hu Huanyong proposed in 1935 that if China was divided into two parts, with the Aihui-Tengchong line as the boundary, the basic pattern of the geographical distribution of the Chinese population would show that 95 percent of the population live in the southeastern half and 5 percent live in the northwestern half, mostly in arid and semi-arid areas. Such was the situation in the 1930s, and it is almost the same at present. The poverty and ignorance of a considerable part of the 35 million people in China who live in poor conditions at present are closely related to their extremely bad living conditions. It is difficult to solve the problem of overpopulation in some areas of China by relying on large-scale domestic immigration. The development of hilly areas for cultivation after the farmland on the plains became insufficient to support the population took place in the mid-20th century. If serious consideration is not given to the resources environment and social and economic conditions, future population growth can only proceed within the given living space. Under huge population pressure, acts of harming the environment, such as destroying forests for land reclamation and lumber, and excessive grazing on the pastureland will be hard to avoid. Therefore, we can easily imagine the deterioration of the quality of life.

The population carrying capacity of the environment cannot be ignored. Today, the international community tends to think that this refers to the non-destruction of the ecological environment and guaranteeing that finite resources can be used permanently and ensuring the maximum population figure for sustainable development. It is difficult to fully determine the environmental capacity because of many uncertain factors. At present, many Chinese scholars hold that the country's maximum population carrying capacity may be 1.5 to 1.6 billion. China has made great efforts to control its population precisely because it is unwilling to see the enlargement of the population exceed the maximum limit permitted by its own resources and environment, and wants to avoid fundamental damage to the living quality of the Chinese population and to ensure sustainable development of the society. China's fundamental population-control policy has been applauded by the majority of natural and social scientists.

The relatively limited per capita possession of natural resources is an objective fact, and the relative shortage of resources arising from the growing population pressure is becoming more and more acute. This has caused damage to the natural material foundation for the survival and development of the Chinese nation.

As is well known, the absolute quantity of China's natural resources ranks among those of the top countries in the world, but because of the large population, the per capita amount is small. The country uses only 7 percent of the world's farmland to feed 22 percent of the world's population. By the end of 2000, China had a little more than 126 million hectares of farmland, but the per capita farmland was only 0.1 hectare, about 45 percent of the world's per capita farmland. In about one-third of the provinces and municipalities, the per capita farmland is less than one-fifteenth of a hectare. The acute shortage of farmland resources and the excessive growth of the population have produced a sharp contradiction. Moreover, industry, transport and large-scale capital construction in both the cities and the countryside use up a lot of land, mostly fertile farmland. As a result, the per capita farmland has dropped year by year. At present, the per capita forest area in China is less than one-seventh of a hectare, and the per capita forest reserve is only nine cubic meters. The per capita grassland in China is only one-third of the world's per capita area and the per capita forest area is only one-fifth of the world's figure. As compared with the forest cover rate of 8.6 percent in the early mid-20th century, China's present forest cover rate has risen to 16.5 percent, but is still far below the world's average of 27 percent. China's water resources total about 2,800 billion cubic meters per year, ranking sixth in the world, but the per capita amount of water is less than 2,200 cubic meters, only one-fourth of the world's per capita amount. Generally speaking, the total amount of resources in a given period is relatively stable. Therefore, the continued population growth will inevitably increase the negative effect of the denominator, forcing the per capita amount of resources down continually.

At the same time, the continued growth of the population has also exerted great pressure on the environment. There are indications that the current population of China has already approached or in some regions has even exceeded the limit of the carrying capacity of the ecological system. For example, the continued growth of the population in modern times has sharpened the contradiction between the growing population and the decreasing farmland with each passing day, and the per capita amount of farmland has dropped year by year. There is already overpopulation in some parts of the country. As a result, in addition to the destruction of forests for reclamation and excessive felling of trees, existing problems include soil erosion, water loss and land desertification. Many poverty-stricken areas are experiencing a vicious circle of "the poorer the people are, the more land is reclaimed; the more land is reclaimed, the poorer the people are."

The continued growth of the population has inevitably been accompanied by the swelling of basic demand, posing the danger of "draining the pond to catch the fish" and "killing the hen to get the eggs." At the same time, it will lead to a shortage of resources and further worsening of the environment. It is obvious that if China cannot check population growth swiftly, nor quickly put an end to excessive tree felling, loss of water and soil, encroachment on farmland and pollution of the environment over large areas, a serious environmental disaster will be inevitable, greatly threatening the minimum living conditions of the great majority of the Chinese people as well as future social and economic development.

Because of the large population and the limitations by other historical conditions, the overwhelming imperative in China for a long time has been the question of survival, the food problem and the problem of how to meet the consumption demands of the huge population. It is said that "People regard food as their primary want." The importance of farmland to an agricultural country is self-evident. The problem is that it will be difficult to avoid the tendency for the population to increase and farmland to decrease in the foreseeable future. Therefore, China cannot but depend more and more on raising the per-unit yield to increase food production to meet the growing demand of its billion-plus population. China's per-unit yield is already far above the world's average, and it will not be easy to further increase the per-unit yield on the basis of the current farming methods and scientific and technological level. According to predictions, even if there should be an optimistic estimate of the increased food production, because of the denominator effect of the big population growth, the average food consumption of the majority of the Chinese people will remain at a fairly low level for a long time.[4]

Of course, the pressure of the consumption demand of the Chinese population is not limited to food. The annual increase of ten million or more newborns devours a huge part of the national income every year (a rough estimate of 30 billion *yuan*). This hampers efforts to improve the living standards of the present population. The huge pressure of the consumption demand inevitably affects accumulation, and then affects many aspects of social and economic development.

In short, the introduction of family planning to control the population growth as a major decision policy conforms to the national conditions in China.

(2) The Historical Evolution of Population Growth in China

We have no choice but to create our new history on the basis of the current large population. The study of the issue of population growth in China specially needs a historical consciousness. Reviewing the history of Chinese population growth, it is not difficult to find two basic characteristics: namely, accelerated progressive increase and cyclic fluctuation. First, China's population fluctuated between 50 million and 70 million from the second year of the Yuanshi reign period of Emperor Ping of the Western Han Dynasty (AD 2) to around 1650 in the reign of Emperor Shunzhi of the Qing Dynasty. Sometimes it even dropped to about 10 million. After the middle of the 17th century, the Chinese population began its continued growth, surpassing 100 million in 1686, 200 million in 1762, 300 million in 1790 and 400 million in 1843. It took 1,600 years for the population to rise from 50 million in AD 2 to 100 million, 76 years from 100 million to 200 million, and 72 years from 200 million to 400 million. To sum up, China's population growth experienced five peak periods historically. The period from the Western Han Dynasty (206 BC to AD 220) to the Wei and Jin dynasties (220-420) was the first peak period, during which the population was between 30 million and 50 million. The period from the Southern and Northern Dynasties (420-589) to the Five Dynasties (907-960) was the second peak period, during which the population stayed between 16 million and 50 million. The period from the Song Dynasty (960-1279) to the Ming Dynasty (1368-1644) saw the third peak, when the population was between 50 million and 63 million. The more than 200 years of the Qing Dynasty saw the population rise shar-

sharply from more than 100 million to 400 million. This was the fourth peak period of China's population growth. The population soared after the founding of the People's Republic of China in 1949. It has risen from more than 500 million in the early 1950s to nearly 1.3 billion at present. It can be said, perhaps, that the Chinese population is now in the middle of the fifth growth peak period. It is estimated that 300 million more newborns will be added during this period. Historically, the cyclical fluctuations of the Chinese population were due to the complex internal relations between the population and politics, economy and culture, as well as the natural environment. Material production, human reproduction and cultural development require mutual coordination, and determine the process of operation of the mega-system of the population.[5]

In the traditional agricultural society, the relationship between man and nature is the foundation for the relations between man and man, and it is manifested mainly in the relationship between man and the land. Around the mid-18th century, China's continued population growth approached a crisis. The land needed to feed the available population was greater than the available farmland.[6] In theory, each society has a constant for food and clothing determined by the level of the productive forces, namely the "hunger and cold boundary." However, under the economic conditions of low productivity, the slow and continued growth of the population often surpassed this bottom line. The non-population factors like the feudal exploitation system (such as the usury practiced by officials and frequent wars) aggravated the concentration of farmland, food grains and other wealth, thus accelerating the process of surpassing the "hunger and cold boundary." By the mid-19th century, the agricultural economy of China collapsed with the outbreak of a new peasant rebellion, namely the "Taiping Revolution." In Guangxi, where the Taiping Revolution broke out, in 1851, the per-hectare yield of farmland was only 4.48 kilograms, because of natural calamities and social upheavals, only 46 percent of the average per-hectare yield of the whole country.[7]

Thus, when the pioneering industrialized countries like Britain began to get out of the "population pitfall" in the mid-19th century, in the prelude to modernization, China's population growth reached its historical peak of feudal society and farming tended to decline step by step. However, the social and economic foundation that maintained the high birth rate remained unchanged. Under the dual shackles of the feudal system and the farming economy, China started to suffer from an excess population.

The population pressure aggravated the impasse of feudal society. First, the contradiction between the large population and the insufficient farmland led to the excessive intensification of the labor force, thus causing a decrease in marginal labor productivity and in marginal remuneration. As a result, the Chinese rural economy was locked in a vicious circle of the dual crises of population growth and reduced efficiency.

Second, the population pressure caused a pathological change in the rural economy. 1) Peasants had to depend on sideline occupations to reorganize their family income, thus promoting the integration of small-scale agriculture and household commodity handicraft production. Nevertheless, the household production structure combining both farming and handicrafts in modern Chinese society brought the re-production of material means and the reproduction of population more closely together, thus solidifying the traditional birth pattern with partiality for male babies, more births and more babies as its essence. As a result, the relations between the population and the economy were bogged down into an unbreakable vicious circle. 2) The small-scale peasant economy became semi-bankrupt. Most of the peasants became impoverished and formed a typical poor small-scale peasant economy. The growth rate of the population kept pace at least with the growth rate of food production. The industry and commerce in the Chinese cities, which had budded at a very early period, lost the opportunity to develop further, and declined due to lack of support from an agricultural surplus. The unprecedented population growth became an important factor preventing China entering the early period of modernization at this time.

Third, the population pressure forced living standards down to the bottom limit of the life-maintaining economy — under the "hunger and cold" boundary line. When the material support force of society reached its limit, the proportion between population growth and natural resources became unbalanced. This natural contradiction inevitably evolved into a social contradiction between man and man. With the growth of the population, material expansion throughout the country reached the limit of that time and could only meet the minimum food supply. There was no agricultural surplus to cope with any contingency (natural calamity or man-made disaster). By the mid-19th century, all parts of the country were troubled by overpopulation, and migration could no longer solve the famine problem; in fact, migration exacerbated it. It was almost impossible to regulate food supply among the different parts of the country, and the choice for the impoverished people was to either await death or rise in rebellion. Scholars have pointed out that population growth exceeding social supply is a catalyst for social upheavals.

The time when two great peasant uprisings (those of the White Lotus Sect and the Taiping Heavenly Kingdom) that sapped the vitality of the Qing Dynasty occurred was precisely the peak period of population growth, and the Chinese population as a whole was under the "hunger and cold" boundary line. It has been estimated that there were 2,332 social upheavals during the ten years from 1856 to 1865.[8] The correlation between population pressure and the upheavals in that century is an important characteristic in modern Chinese history that cannot be ignored.

Why did the Chinese population keep growing after the 17th century? The early phase (1644-1865) of the Qing Dynasty saw the fastest growth of the Chinese population in the feudal society that lasted for more than two thousand years. The growth of the population from more than 100 million in 1691 to 400 million in 1841 directly laid the foundation for the modern size of the Chinese population. In the following chapters, we will study the general historical foundation for the high birth rate — the small peasant economy, the traditional birth culture and the given historical conditions, for example, the changes in the tax and corvée system during the prosperous reigns of the early to middle Qing Dynasty.

(3) Solving the Historical Enigma of Population Growth in China: the Viewpoint of Social Demography

China is a country with more mountains than farmland. The Central Plain region is locked in by the Yanshan, Taihang, Dabie, Wuyi, Qinling and the Nanling mountain ranges on the north, west and south. To the east of the plain lie the

Bohai, Yellow and East China seas. The Central Plain was the cradle of a flourishing agricultural civilization, but could never provide the historical conditions for the development of a commodity economy. Even during the Qing Dynasty, when the population rose and the country's territory expanded, the Gobi and other deserts, the high mountains in Siberia, the Mongolian Highlands and Central Asia still blocked China's cultural field of view.

Therefore, China was dominated by a fully developed small-scale peasant economy for many centuries. The small-scale peasant economy consists of households as the basic production units and childbearing units. The marriage between the small-scale peasant economy and the patriarchal clan system created the essence and basic spirit of traditional Chinese culture, and forcefully restricted the value-orientation of the Chinese people in regard to life, family and society. The reproduction of the population, as the basic prerequisite for survival, was also controlled by it.

In such a society, the purpose and significance of life seemed to be entirely to bear the obligation of devoting oneself to one's family. The value of life was, first of all, to procreate the human groups with the households as units and bring them honor. To produce children was not regarded as up to individual preference, but as a duty, especially the producing of sons to carry on the family name. The will and sense of value of an individual were suppressed. The will of the family head and the interests of the family were supreme, and were in fact termed "heavenly principles". To have sons from generation to generation was regarded as a matter of primary importance to the worship of ancestors and the continuation of the family line. This was the most important part of "filial piety".

The ethical system with filial piety as the core long exerted a subtle influence on the cultural and psychological structure of the Chinese nation. It was said that "there are three disloyal acts, and the greatest of them all is not to have a son to carry on the family line." This moral imperative became ingrained in the Chinese mentality over a period of millennia.

The struggle for survival propelled feudal families to seek to give birth to as many children as possible. In addition, with the intention of making the country rich and building up military might (because the population was the source of taxes and recruits), the rulers of all dynasties regarded manpower as national strength, taking measures to encourage population growth. Even today this "historical hand" is still at work in some of China's poverty-stricken and underdeveloped regions.

The basic characteristic of traditional Chinese farming was that under primitive and backward production and technical conditions, increased farm output depended on the increase of labor input, apart from the natural conditions of favorable weather. It can even be said that the input of human power was the biggest investment in the traditional farming economy. Therefore, rapid reproduction was regarded as desirable. The wishes at wedding celebrations included "Have a son as soon as possible" and "To have more sons is to have more blessings." In brief, the small-scale peasant economy with the family as the basic production unit had a natural impulse to increase the population size. The inherent weakness of this farming economy determined the unique value of manpower in its lasting and difficult contention with the forces of Nature. The farming pattern of "depending on Heaven for food" has a long history in China.

Whether during the heyday of the Han and Tang dynasties or that of the Kangxi reign period of the Qing Dynasty, the farming economy depended on Nature, and the ability to resist natural calamities had always been very small, while the ability to resist man-made calamities was even smaller. On this question, Dr. Huang Zongzhi, in his book *The Small-scale Peasant Economy and Social Vicissitudes in North China*, gives a factual description: "A drought in one year meant three years of predicaments. Droughts in two successive years meant land rent burden and misery for the rest of the farmer's life. The poor peasants were like a man in neck-deep water; even a small wave might drown him."[9] This subsistence economy determined the relative balance between the high mortality rate and the simple reproduction of the population with a high birth rate.

In the feudal natural economic system, land was the major source for the self-sufficient small-scale peasant economy. In order to meet the demand for food by the growing population, on the one hand, the area of farmland was expanded without limit, and even hills and mountains were reclaimed and cultivated. In the Qing Dynasty (1644-1911), the area of farmland greatly increased. As mentioned above, the area of cultivated farmland throughout the country totaled about 818,000 hectares in the early years of the Qing Dynasty, and was extended to 1.165 million hectares by the Qianlong reign period (1736-1795). In fact, in the first half of the 20th century, there were already very few land resources left for reclamation. On the other hand, the intensification of agricultural management reached a very high level, and the increased labor power assembled on the limited farmland and the intensive farming reached the highest degree. History shows that in the Warring States Period (475-221 BC),

China's agricultural management had already changed from extensive farming to labor-intensive farming at the level of the productive forces of the time. It is a pity, however, that agricultural production developed very slowly in the next 2,000 years and more. During the middle and late years of the Warring States Period, per hectare yield of food grains in China was already 1,620 kilograms. By the Tang Dynasty (618-907), it had risen to 2,505 kilograms. It rose again to 2,752.5 kilograms in the early and middle periods of the Qing Dynasty (1644-1911). These were the highest yields ever attained with traditional agricultural techniques.[10] According to Dr. Huang Zongzhi's book, *The Small-scale Peasant Economy and Social Vicissitudes in North China*, a Chinese family in the 19th and early 20th century had an average of five members, including two able-bodied members, with each able-bodied person capable of cultivating 1 to 2 hectare of farmland.[11] During the whole period of the Qing Dynasty, the per-capita farmland fluctuated between 0.1 and 0.5 hectare.[12] This showed the high degree of intensification of farming and the different degrees of labor surpluses of the ordinary farm households.

However, apart from the reason stated above, there were specific historical conditions and turning points accounting for the rapid growth of the Chinese population in the last few centuries of the feudal society.

First, the improvement of census data. The common people often concealed the number of their family members in order to evade taxes and corvée. Therefore, censuses taken before the Qianlong reign period (before 1736) were often below the actual figure.

Second, the introduction of sorghum, sweet potatoes and other high-yield crops provided alternative food sources, and a better guarantee for the livelihood of the new generation. And the new round of population growth further increased the demand for food, leading to the increased demand for additional labor input and further stimulating the multiplication of the population. John King Fairbanks said in his book *The United States and China* that the increased food production eased the people's suffering in the famine years, increased the people's resistance to illness, and brought the positive results of reduced infant mortality, thus enabling most of the female babies to survive to have children."[13]

Third, during the Kangxi (1662-1722) and Qianlong (1736-1795) reign periods, people lived longer and the harvests were good. Emperor Kangxi announced in 1712 that "no taxes will be levied on newborns from now on." He again definitely stipulated that from the 51st year (1713) of his reign "Household registration will become permanent. The newly increased population will be reported on the basis of the actual figures, but no taxes will be added forever." After the middle of the Qianlong reign period, repeated orders were issued to implement the stipulation of the above decrees. In the first year (1723) of the Yongzheng reign period a new measure was taken to collect taxes on the basis of the amount of farmland owned by each family, instead of the number of members in each family. The new measure replaced the poll tax, which had helped to check the population growth. From then on, the Chinese population began to grow at an annual average rate of 25 percent. At the same time, more and more wasteland was reclaimed. This helped the population growth keep a relative balance against the shortage of cultivable land.

Fourth, the feudal society had no positive social or economic mechanism for checking the excessive growth of the population, nor did it have the possibility of having one. Even in times of peace and prosperity, it could not extricate itself from the vicious circle. During the Qianlong reign period, there were few extra land resources for reclamation, and there was almost no improvement in the production techniques, but the rapid growth of the population was unchecked. The contradiction between the population growth and the natural resources often evolved into social upheavals and change of dynasties, and initiated a new cycle of evolution.

Fifth, the frequent social upheavals sometimes also obstructed the vision of the people. In a society inflicted with all kinds of ills, people often lost their alertness against the hidden pressure from the precipitous population growth. A look at the first hundred years of modern Chinese history reveals a picture of "social upheavals, domestic troubles and foreign invasions." The Qing Dynasty in the last years of the feudal society had no spare energy to cope with the "population problem." Under the pressure of foreign invasions, national defense naturally became the most urgent priority. Whether it was Gong Zizhen's "theory of immigration", or Wang Shiduo's "theory of birth control" or Yan Fu's "theory of evolution, their concern with "the problem of having too many people" raised only a ripple of concern in the modern Chinese realm of ideology.[14] The sociological polemic on the population problem set off by population pressure in the 1930s discussed this problem for the first time against the historical background of "modernization", but it neither aroused the attention of the ruling group nor a wide response from society at large.

It is worth noting that the population growth during the "flourishing period of the Kangxi and Qianlong reign periods" constituted the historical latent point for the skyrocketing of the Chinese population in the second half of the 20th century, together with its unique problems. Before the founding of the People's Republic of China opened a new era of development in China, traditional agriculture had, in fact, already become intensified and reached the critical point for the progressive decrease of marginal returns. The small-scale peasant economy had developed to the stage of being restricted by resources, and the rapid growth of the population had exerted a strong negative impact, in contrast to the social and economic development. For example, it was no longer rare to see the population growth rate exceed the growth rate of grain production and farmland expansion, and labor intensification exceed the decrease of marginal remuneration.[15]

However, the industrialization movement bred in the newly established People's Republic of China under the conditions of the new relations of production and organizational system once again covered up the "population problem". The three years of land reform (from the winter of 1950 to the spring of 1953) gave more than 300 million peasants who had had little or no farmland about 466,000 hectares of farmland, draught animals and farm implements. Pauperization in rural areas was therefore checked, and the farm production was gratifyingly expanded in scale. By 1956, the Chinese government had initially solved the problem of unemployment for four million urban residents left behind by the old society. According to an investigation conducted by the labor department in some cities in May 1956, skilled workers constituted less than 5 percent of the jobless in the cities.[16] The population problem seemed to have gone away. At the same time, China's population growth also passed a historical turning point. Thanks to the constantly improving living conditions and rapidly developing medical service, the human mortality rate after national liberation in 1949 dropped much faster than the average rate in developing countries. Hardly had the birth rate had time to respond, when China reached a period of rapid growth of population, just like the sudden "baby boom" after World War II. Between 1950 and 1970, the annual natural growth rate of the Chinese population was as high as 25 per thousand on average, and even neared 30 per thousand in exceptional years. By 1982, when the third national census was conducted, the population on the Chinese mainland had surpassed one billion. In less than one-third of a century, the Chinese population had doubled. As compared with the last cycle of doubling the population, this cycle was completed in less than one-third of the time. When the fourth national census was conducted in 1990, the Chinese population had risen to 1.133 billion. Now it is approaching 1.3 billion.

It should be seen that the continued existence of the small-scale peasant economy and the formation of the dual urban and rural social and economic pattern were the primary social and economic factors in the rapid growth of the population after the founding of the People's Republic. This is perhaps the fundamental reason why the population growth was not actively checked after the process of China's modernization accelerated its transformation. In fact, from the founding of the People's Republic to the beginning of the economic reform in the late 1970s, Chinese agriculture evolved basically along the road of labor-intensive development with extensive cultivation, and the change of the social system did not fundamentally transform the basic structure of the farming economy, which was a predominantly small-scale peasant economy. As a result, the mechanism for

China's population growth could not have been changed from the spontaneous pattern to the restrictive pattern earlier.

This change of mechanism began in the late 1970s, showing that China has finally realized the necessity of maintaining the harmonious relations of adaptation and coordination among population growth, economic development and environmental changes after paying a huge historical price. It also shows that China has the ability to regulate the process of population change by various means, and has taken vigorous steps forward in coordinating the relations between population growth and social and economic development.

Chapter 2

The Population Problem New China Faced

(1) The Population Growth and the Views on Population Before 1980

There was only an approximate figure of 475 million for the total national population when the People's Republic of China was founded in 1949. At that time, socialist construction needed a lot of manpower. At the same time, China still had a lot of land and other resources to be developed and utilized. Therefore, the population problem did not attract wide attention for the time being.

According to data collected during the first national census in modern times, taken in 1953, the Chinese population was 540 million, accounting for 22 percent of the world population. By 1954, the population had surpassed the 600-million mark. At that time, the Chinese population, just like that of other developing countries, had entered the period of transitional growth momentum. That is, the birth rate rose rapidly while the mortality rate dropped dramatically. As a result, the natural growth of the population was greatly accelerated. In fact, family planning had already started in some areas (chiefly in cities). Because of complicated historical reasons, no policy was formulated, and the opportunity to rein in the population increase was lost.

Beginning in 1962, the Chinese population reached its second peak since the founding of the People's Republic. According to UN statistics, the average total birth rate of Chinese women in the 1960s was 5.96, higher than the average rate in Asia and Latin America, and nearly the same as in Africa, South Asia and West Asia. In the late 1960s, the average annual growth rate of the Chinese population was as high as 2.61 percent, even higher than in Africa and South Asia, which had the highest rates, but a little lower than in West Asia. Between 1960 and 1975, China had an average of 27.3 million newborns a year — a total of 410 million newborns — showing an increase of 270 million. Between 1965 and 1975, China's net population increase equaled the total population of the United States. It is true that in the second birth peak period, the rapid growth of the Chinese population had something to do with the high birth rate of 33 per thousand for many years, but its main reason was that the mortality rate in China dropped faster than in most developing countries. For example, between 1949 and 1957 China's mortality rate dropped from 20 per thousand to 10.8 per thousand, and it dropped further from 9.5 per thousand to 7.6 per thousand from 1965 to 1970. This greatly accelerated the population growth. Because the total mortality rate level dropped quickly from the late 1950s and the birth rate was kept at a fairly high level, the natural population growth rate rose rapidly until the early 1970s. Except in the three years of economic difficulties (1961-1963), the natural growth rate of the Chinese population maintained the high level of above 20 per thousand. At the same time, the marked fall of the mortality rate also showed the remarkable achievement China had made in protecting the right of existence of its huge population. The reason why China's mortality rate dropped faster than that in most developing countries is that, apart from the progress in medical skills after World War II which brought contagious diseases menacing the health of the mankind under effective control throughout the world, China carried out the work of sanitation, health protection, prevention and treatment of diseases on a mass scale, the living standards of the people were improved after the founding of the People's Republic, and distribution of economic materials was relatively equal. All this visibly forced down the mortality rate of the Chinese people.

Because more people were born and the period of the second human birth peak lasted longer, it was difficult to alleviate and eliminate the inertia of population growth over a short period of time. The Chinese population had surpassed the 800-million mark by 1969, and it exceeded the 900-million mark in the mid-1970s. It is estimated that no matter what strict measures China takes its population in the mid-21st century will peak at the figures of 1.5 to 1.6 billion. If efforts are relaxed even a little, the Chinese population could be two billion by that time.

In 1949, China had 100 million hectares of farmland, an average of 0.18 hectare per capita, already below the world average level. At the end of 1956, the Chinese population was 620 million, and 15.9 percent of them had been born after the founding of the People's Republic in 1949. In fact, before 1956, the rural areas already had a surplus of laborers. According to a survey taken in Hejian County, Hebei Province, the rate of annual field attendance of an individual peasant in 1950 was generally 110-112 days for a man and around 30 days for a woman. A survey of 26,000 agricultural cooperatives in 1955 showed that an able-bodied person worked 96 days a year on average, and there was plenty of spare time for the peasants. In Xianghe and other counties in Hebei Province, the surplus labor in the agricultural cooperatives was about 26 percent in the period 1955-1956. In 18 agricultural cooperatives in Yanggao, Lingqiu and three other counties in Shanxi Province, about 30 percent of the labor force was idle. In 18 agricultural cooperatives in Neijiang County, Sichuan Province, the surplus labor accounted for 35 percent of the total.[17] By that time, government leaders and some realistic scholars had realized the challenge and pressure from the excessive growth of the population. Historical documents show that top leaders Deng Xiaoping, Liu Shaoqi, Zhou Enlai and Mao Zedong spoke of birth control with approval. In the autumn of 1953, Deng Xiaoping was the first to speak of the need to "practice birth control".[18] In the winter of the following year, Liu Shaoqi said explicitly, when he presided over a meeting on birth control: "Now we must say definitely that the Party favors birth control." He also gave specific instructions on abortion, sterilization and the supply of contraceptives.[19] On March 1, 1955, the Central Committee of the Communist Party of China pointed out in its remarks on the report on the question of birth control submitted by the Ministry of Public Health: "Birth control is a question of major policy concerning the life of the broad masses of the people. In the present historical conditions, for the happiness of the nation, the families and the new-born generation, our Party approves appropriate birth control." In September 1956, Zhou Enlai pointed out at the Eighth National Congress of the Communist Party of China: "In order to protect women and children, and bring up our later generations very well in the interest of the health and prosperity of the nation, we favor appropriate birth control." In 1957, Chairman Mao Zedong even explicitly proposed the concept of "family planning" and the idea of "introducing family planning throughout the country step by step".[20]

It is worth noting that Dr. Ma Yinchu, a noted economist and president of Peking University, who was an outstanding representative of the Chinese intellectuals at that time, conducted surveys in his native county, Shengxian, Zhejiang Province, three times during the period 1954-1955. He found an astonishingly high birth rate. He thus warned: "If the Chinese population grows like this, unchecked, it will surely become an obstacle to the development of the productive forces."[21] He pointed out that the excessive growth of the population would cause the following problems: One, contradiction with the accelerated capital accumulation; two, contradiction with the rise of labor productivity; three, contradiction with the improvement of the people's livelihood; and four, contradiction with the development of science. He further said: "China has little financial resources and a big population. It is not bad to organize the people, and make use of them as a resource. But don't forget that the big population is also a large burden. My new population theory holds that we retain its advantage and get rid of its disadvantage, save the large resource and remove the large burden. The method is to improve the quality and control the quantity of the population."[22] Dr. Ma's "New Population Theory" advocated regular censuses, birth control and contraception. He held the view that the quality and quantity of the population must be properly harmonized. However, his proposals were cold-shouldered.

The high rate of economic growth, to a degree, covered up the latent danger of the fast growth of the population. At the time, some people held the view that, with the development of economic construction and especially of the socialist

28

sector in China, the Chinese population would increase considerably, and this increase would be favorable for large-scale economic construction. Another view was that under the socialist system a bigger population should not be understood as a bigger natural pressure, but as a greater social productive force. In short, the dominant thought on population at the time was that the continual growth of the population was regarded as a manifestation of socialist superiority, and that to practice family planning and birth control was "new Malthusianism" that departed from the accepted doctrine.

It should be seen that the existence of the small-scale peasant economy was the historical "hotbed" for the rapid growth of the population after the founding of New China and also the fundamental cause for the failure to vigorously check the growth of the population. In other words, the socio-economic and cultural factors for the change of the traditional birth pattern were insufficiently developed. The development of the Chinese agricultural economy in the 1950s basically inherited the extensive farming mainly characterized by the expansion of resources. During the years from 1949 to 1957, some 1.4 million hectares of new farmland was added. While the per-unit yield dropped, the total grain output increased by more than 5 million kilograms as a result of the extension of the sown area. At the same time, however, the rural labor force grew by more than 20 million. This produced tension between population growth and increase of grain production, and hampered attempts to reform the traditional small-scale peasant economy.

It should also been seen that the dual urban and rural social and economic pattern kept a large part of the fast-growing population in the villages, and the progress made in urban industrialization did not reduce the relative portion of the rural population. The traditional type of human reproduction in the rural areas could not change into the modern type. Before the reform policy was introduced in the late 1970s, the near-equalitarian rural distribution system also encouraged peasant families to have more children. For example, Sichuan Province once introduced the distribution system of "seven to three for the major part, and eight to two for the minor part." This meant that 70 percent of the food grain was distributed on the basis of the number of persons in each family, and 30 percent on the basis of the work points each contributed. Of the latter percentage, 20 percent was distributed on the basis of the manure contributed by each family in terms of work points. The natural employment system practiced in the rural areas (namely, a person reaching the legal work age or even below was entitled to work in the production sphere without having to go through any procedure or paying any price. In return he received remuneration) also encouraged ordinary peasant households to seek higher economic returns by having more children. The striking contrast between the expected returns from children and the cost of fostering children determined their desire to have more children, and their partiality for boys.

The characteristics of the growth of the Chinese population after the founding of the People's Republic were: One, high speed. Between 1949 and 1982, the annual natural growth rate of the population was as high as 19 per thousand. Two, severe fluctuation. The first population growth peak after the founding of the People's Republic was seen between 1952 and 1957, with an annual average natural growth rate being higher than 20 per thousand. The growth rate dropped in the period from 1958 to 1961, and there was even a negative growth in 1960. This was an effect on the population operation mechanism produced by the "Great Leap Forward" and the three years of natural calamities. China experienced its second human growth peak in the period from 1962 to 1973, with an annual natural growth rate of above 20 per thousand, and the peak lasted for as long as 12 years. The natural growth rate dropped year by year in the 1970s, and it was under 20 per thousand between 1974 and the early 1980s. This was mainly attributed to the determined efforts made in family planning.

(2) Family Planning in China: a Discussion on the Historical Basis

Since China began to practice family planning vigorously in the early 1970s, it has made great achievements. International experts have unanimously acknowledged that China has been one of the most successful countries in controlling population growth. Through more than twenty years of painstaking efforts, the birth rate and the natural population growth rate have dropped visibly. From 1970 to 1995, the birth rate dropped from 33.43 per thousand to 17.12 per thousand, and the natural growth rate from 25.83 per thousand to 10.55 per thousand. According to data provided by the United Nations, it is certain that the Chinese population growth rate is lower than the average figure in the developing countries. In 1995, in other developing countries, the average population growth rate was 31 per thousand, the average natural growth rate was 22 per thousand, and the average total birth rate was 4. The effective family planning campaign has created conditions conducive to the country's reform and opening up drive, promoting social and economic development, and guaranteeing the right of existence and development of the huge Chinese population.

There was a rich historical background and a solid historical foundation for the family planning efforts. The review above shows that the formal implementation of the family planning policy in the 1970s originated from sound knowledge of the facts. This is the first point.

Second, the vigorous introduction of family planning in China from the late 1970s had a good mass foundation and work foundation established in the 1960s and 1970s.

In the early years after the founding of the People's Republic, more and more women in the cities were released from household tasks, and took part in economic construction. Many families accepted contraception and birth control. With the passage of time and social and economic development, more and more Chinese women became receptive to birth control.

Before family planning was introduced in an all-round way in the 1970s, there was already a good foundation for the family planning work. The main manifestations were: 1) The establishment and improvement of the organizational setup. For example, the All-China Medical Association set up a birth control technical guidance committee, with noted gynecologist Lin Qiaozhi as its chairwoman in March 1957. The State Council set up the Family Planning Commission in January 1964. 2) More contraceptives and birth control techniques were produced and made available. The Ministry of Public Health called a national meeting to share technical experiences in family planning and introduce preliminary birth control techniques in January 1964. The State Science and Technology Commission, the Ministry of Public Health and the Ministry of Fuel and the Chemical Industry jointly called a national meeting in Shanghai to appraise and promote five kinds of quick-action oral contraceptives in June 1967. 3) Increasing publicity was given to contraception, birth control, and promotion of good prenatal and postnatal care in the cities and rural areas step by step. The Ministry of Public Health issued the "Directives on Contraception Work" on August 6, 1956, in accordance with an instruction from the Central Government and in light of the development of the situation, and gave wide publicity to it. From then on, wide publicity was given to scientific knowledge about contraception, contraception methods and birth control techniques. At the same time, the supply of contraceptives and related quality inspection were improved. The Ministry of Public Health also simplified the procedure for induced abortion and sterilization operations. The Family Planning Commission under the State Council called an on-the-spot meeting to share experiences in late marriage and birth control in Wendeng County, Shandong Province, known nationwide for its experience in this respect, in February 1965.

It was in the early 1970s that the Central Government made up its mind to exert great efforts to introduce family planning, because it realized that the continued high growth of the population after 1962 had so aggravated economic difficulties that it must be tackled.

The Chinese population surpassed the 800-million mark in 1969, and rose to 830 million in the following year. The unchecked fast growth of the population brought the national economy to the brink of collapse, and pauperization in rural areas could hardly be held back, with hundreds of millions of people living below the absolute poverty line (According to government statistics, there were 250 million absolutely poor people in 1978, who could not properly feed or clothe themselves). From 1957 to 1970, the per-capita farmland in China dropped from 0.17 hectare to 0.12 hectare. At the same time, the per-capita grain output dropped from 307 kilograms to 293 kilograms.[23] The majority of Chinese people kept themselves fed and clothed at a low level. The tremendous employment pressure also haunted governments at all levels. On the one hand, the surplus labor force in rural areas kept increasing. In fact, before 1956, the rural areas were already saturated with labor or even had surpluses. On the other hand, the number of jobs available in cities and towns could hardly meet the growing demand for employment. As a result, there was a serious urban unemployment problem. In the same year, the large-scale movement to send young school graduates to work in the countryside and mountainous areas was a reflection of this problem. The countryside and agriculture became a huge "reservoir" for the growing surplus labor force, but the agricultural foundation was also continuously weakened as a result of the progressive decrease of marginal utility. If agriculture were not stable, the national economy would not be stable either. Later, the people's commune system as an extremely strong social integrating force prevented the emergence of a huge migration problem, but the organizational benefit from this innovative organizational form was far from being able to offset the prodigious waste of human resources resulting from low efficiency. The marginal return rate of agriculture was extremely low, even zero or negative at times. Before long, the mode of collective labor not only disguised increasing accumulation of surplus labor force, but even created false labor shortage (for example, during the "Great Leap Forward"). As a result, the urgency of population control disappeared from the top-level policy-making process. In the urban-rural dichotomy, China had no mechanism for the normal movement of rural labor force to back modern economic growth. The quiet huge growth of the rural population further increased the pressure of overpopulation. The situation of growing population, decreasing farmland and food shortages went from bad to worse, and "hunger" became commonplace. The outstanding food and employment problems finally made the government aware of the huge pressure of the rapidly growing population. Premier Zhou Enlai repeatedly pointed out that it would soon be too late if China did not pay special attention to family planning. In 1971, the State Council brushed aside all kinds of resistance, and began to make new arrangements for the family planning endeavor, and re-established the family planning organ directly under its own leadership in 1973. In the early 1970s, the Chinese government formally included the population growth target in the national economic plan, and formulated the family planning policy of encouraging "late, widely spaced and fewer births," and started to carry out family planning drive both in cities and the countryside step by step. Following the 3rd Plenary Session of the 11th Central Committee of the Communist Party of China, held in late 1978, some scholars further proposed the idea of vigorously pursuing a one-child policy, and firmly stopping couples having more than two children. "Restrict the quantity of the population and improve the quality of the population" as the basic content of the Chinese population policy became gradually clear. Family planning was adopted at the 12th National Congress of the Communist Party of China, held in 1984, as a fundamental state policy.

With family planning introduced on a wider scale and the rising tide of enthusiasm for the reform and opening up program in and after the 1980s, China has further broadened its people's field of vision on the population issue, and become more deeply and fully aware of the necessity of pursuing family planning.

To do a thorough job of family planning, China must not only place emphasis on control of the total quantity of the population, but also on the control of the growth of the working-age population. Those born now will become working-age people demanding work after a certain number of years. With the beginning of the life cycle, there will be a corresponding change in the demand from the population. The total labor force in China was 870 million in the year 2000. The forecast made according to the population simulation model built on the basis of the fifth national census shows that the total supply of laborers in China will continue to rise for the next twenty years or so. By 2013, the active labor force will reach a peak of around 1 billion, and will start to decrease by 2025. However, the percentage of the active labor force will continue to rise, and will remain above the world's average level. The newly active labor force added in 2001 was 11 million, and 14 million were added in 2002. It is true that an abundance of labor force is conducive to development, but due to China's relative shortage of funds and resources, it is extremely difficult to solve the problem of employment of such a large labor force. China has already made gratifying successes in solving this difficult problem by taking a number of measures to create job opportunities, but it is still difficult to put an end to the situation in which the supply of labor force is far greater than demand. China will face huge employment pressure and many challenges arising from this for a fairly long time to come.

First, there will be strong growth momentum for Chinese

labor in the foreseeable future, and the annual increase will exceed 10 million. This will considerably hinder China's efforts to change its industrial structure, consisting mainly of labor-intensive traditional industries, to an industrial structure consisting mainly of capital-intensive and technology-intensive modern industries, thus hampering economic development and social progress. There is no doubt that if the country exercises better control over the population today, there will be fewer difficulties in the future.

Second, because of the serious employment pressure, the contradiction between "fairness" and "efficiency" has long haunted China, and there has been great difficulty in making profound social and economic reforms. On the one hand, China now needs a stable social environment more than ever to promote construction, reform and opening up. If there is any imprudence, it may affect social stability. On the other hand, in order to establish a healthy, really effective economic system, China must introduce a competitive mechanism, give priority to efficiency, and improve the economic outcome of employment. For this reason, it is essential to establish a standard and common labor market to change the past employment system. However, under the present historical conditions, when the socialist market economy is still not fully developed, the psychological bearing capacity of the people is still weak, the labor market is not yet developed and the unemployment insurance and security system remains to be improved, there is a great risk in emphasizing efficiency.

Third, China's employment pressure will mainly come from the growing surplus rural labor. Whether the issue of finding a way out for the hundreds of millions of surplus rural labor can be properly solved is of vital importance to the success of the reform in China's rural areas. Again there is a difficult choice: Let large numbers of peasants swarm into the cities freely with all kinds of harmful consequences arising from it or restrict peasants from going into the cities, with the result of unforeseeable modernization of agriculture and the countryside. Therefore, progress in the family planning work is directly and closely related to the course of and prospects for China's modernization.

The objective of China's development is explicit and definite: to strive to attain the level of the moderately developed countries and build China further into a prosperous, strong, democratic and culturally advanced modern socialist country. An important sign of improvement of the living standards of the people is the rise of per-capita income and per-capita consumption. However, China's efforts have met challenges from two aspects: On the one hand, the low production capacity and the relative shortage of resources determine that China's GNP and production of many major products will not be high for a fairly long period of time; and on the other, as the total population is already too big and continues to grow, the per-capita levels of income, output and consumption will not be high for many years to come. China has focused on economic construction, launched reforms, opened the country further to the outside world, and established a socialist market economic system precisely for the sake of solving its low production capacity and relative shortage of resources, and has already made gratifying achievements. China has made great efforts to practice family planning to slow down the speed of population growth and strive to keep the population growth lower than the growth of the GNP and national wealth, thereby raising the per-capita level step by step.

The improvement of the quality of life and the quality of the population is the most important sign of development. What history has bequeathed to China is a population with excessive quantity and low quality. The two interact as both cause and effect, in a vicious circle. To fundamentally change this situation, China must control the quantity of the population and improve its quality simultaneously. From the viewpoint of the long-time and healthy development of the population, China should consider adjustment of the population structure.

Today, the world has reached a consensus on the stabilization of the global population. As the most populous country in the world, China recognizes that it has particular responsibility for the stabilization of the world population. Therefore, China has made great efforts to practice family planning both for its own vital interests and for the common interests of all the people on the globe. China's efforts for population control are of vital importance to the early stabilization of the world population.

In fact, precisely because of China's effective population control, its population remained stable at 21.5 percent of the global population from 1990 to 2000. China's population control program is an outstanding contribution to the stabilization of the population of the world as a whole.

Overpopulation in China has very profound negative effects. It can be said that it has penetrated all aspects of the country's social and economic life. The solution to all Chinese problems, big or small, is more or less related to the population factor. It can be said that the basic state policy of practicing family planning in an all-round way is a correct policy decision made in the second half of the 20th century that brings benefits for contemporary times and contributes to future generations. Just like the reform and opening up program, it is indispensable for China's development.

Chapter 3

Opportunities and Challenges for the Solution to the Population Problem Brought About by the Reform and Opening up Program

The drastic changes which have taken place in China over the last two decades or so are bound to be reflected in all aspects of the population issue.

First, the market-oriented socio-economic transformation has accumulated much experience. Especially in the 1990s, China made an explicit decision to introduce a socialist market economic system. The revolutionary changes in the economic and social system, and the process of market-oriented transformation have already produced and will continue to produce a profound effect on the population situation and population work. This effect is reflected in many aspects. To begin with, the environment for the subsistence of the Chinese people has begun to be reconstructed in the course of developing the market economy, that is, the gradual change from an environment for subsistence covered by the traditional "family focused" culture to the environment for subsistence with the modern "personal focused" culture as its soul. The traditional thought of the Chinese on reproduction "regardless of cost" has begun to transform. The change of the traditional desire for more babies, the modernization of the birth culture and the realization of the change to a modern population norm are all significant. Second, the development of the market economy inevitably demands the dynamic optimization of the allocation of the essential factors of production, including the working population. The unprecedented upsurge in the population flow, the start of an urbanization movement in the modern sense, and the initial appearance of the trend of "having the country in the town, the town in the country, non-separation of town from country and blending of town and country" presages the inevitable prospect of replacing the dual structure of separating town and country in economic management. Population movement has also brought about new problems. This is not a "blind" movement. With the clear motive of shaking off poverty and seeking prosperity, rural people are flowing into the areas where there are opportunities for prosperity. Third, a great change has also taken place in the countryside. The momentum of rural industrialization and urbanization is very encouraging. This trend can also be called "local urbanization" or "self-urbanization". Rural people have not changed their residences nor their household or identity registration, but their way of making a living, life-style, ideology and values are all undergoing profound changes. All this will inevitably help to change people's notions and behavior as regards marriage and giving birth. More and more Chinese peasants are becoming new-type farmers who are sharing modern urban civilization and getting involved in the process of modernization. All this is changing the mechanism of the Chinese population issue, its way of manifestation and its consequences.

Second, since China began to implement the family planning policy in the early 1970s, it has made great achievements in controlling the population, which has caught worldwide attention. The Chinese population has started a low-growth period under given restrictive conditions. However, while the human birth rate tends to fall, it is still difficult to check the continued swelling of the total population for the time being. While the birth rate has dropped to approach the replacement level (an average of one couple with two children), the periodic increment of the population is still rising because of the growth momentum. This is precisely the phenomenon of "low birth rate and high increment" and has become a fundamental characteristic of the population situation since the beginning of the 1990s, and is different from those of the 1970s and 1980s. This is the first point. Second, the wave of the aged population has arrived as expected, with a powerful surge that should not be slighted. Shanghai, Beijing and other major cities have gradually entered the stage of the aged society. The rapidly increasing proportion of the aged to the whole population and the many problems arising from this constitute one of the major social issues attracting wide attention in China.

Therefore, on the one hand, the external factors that affect the population situation are undergoing great changes. On the other, the inherent law of population operation has led us into a period of more complex population problems. So how can we "choose the lesser of two evils and choose the greater of two goods"?

(1) Population Control in the Era of Market Economy

At present, China is in a special historic period of replacing the old economic structure with a new one. During this period, while the old order is being eliminated, it will take years to establish a new order. Especially, it is impossible to expect the new concepts and new culture to be established and grow quickly within a short period of time. While the new market economic structure is being established, the birth concept and behavior of some people are still affected by tradition or are sandwiched between the traditional and the modern.

Since the market-oriented economic restructuring was started in the early 1990s, the migrant population has grown rapidly. While the movement for the redistribution of the population has become stronger and stronger, the problem of "unplanned births" has inevitably emerged.

A salient feature of the market economy is the optimum allocation of the essential factors of production through the market mechanism. It can be well imagined that, with the development of the commodity market and the factors of production market, population movements will not only be less blind, but more conscious under the guidance of the law of the market economy (different from the much-talked-about "blind influx" of the 1980s). It will become bigger and bigger in scale and scope in order to meet the needs of regulating surpluses and shortages. What is particularly significant is that the pattern of blending urban and rural people on a large scale will gradually take shape. More and more farmers will be involved in the production and sale of commodities to achieve the optimum allocation of the essential factors of production in the dual variation of job transfer (from farming to other trades) and regional transfer (from country to town). The transfer of rural labor from country to town has developed even more quickly like wildfire in recent years following its first tide in the 1980s. At the same time, urbanization in the country has also caught more and more attention.

It should be seen that the growth of the migrating population is an inevitable associated thing of the development of the market economy. It is the objective inevitability of the induction law of the comparative interests. However, the rapid growth of the migrating population may also lead to "unplanned births". In other words, it will still be difficult to control the birth rate of the migrant population.

Change in the concept of desirable family size is of profound significance for the control of the population. The modernization of the birth culture can be defined as the constant growth of the dominant idea of the importance of fewer births or even no births, and the gradual extinction of the idea that the more children one has the better. The effect of the modernization of birth culture on population control is reflected in the ability to reduce the opposition to the control of the population and to help form a self-restraint mechanism for population growth. Of course, the modernization of the birth culture will not be accomplished overnight, nor will it come of itself. There is reason to believe that the modernization of the Chinese birth culture is already being manifested.

The development of the market economy is not conducive to population control in the short term, but development is also a kind of control, and its importance is growing. Therefore, population work has two focal points: 1) Efforts must be made to weaken the factors leading to a rebound of the rural birth rate in the initial growth period of the market economy; and 2) Efforts must be made to cultivate the mechanism of the market economy to restrain the growth of the population. These are two aspects of the same question.

Concretely, emphasis must be placed on the following

aspects in the construction and cultivation of the new mechanism for population control:

First, get more farmers involved more widely and more deeply in the commodity market, factors of production market and property rights market to promote the social disintegration of the farmers and the change of their concepts as regards reproduction.

Generally speaking, the slower the social disintegration, the more complete the traditional form and often the stronger the opposition to population control. "Poverty creates a big population" sums up this phenomenon. With the transfer of more farmers from farming to other trades and the development of urbanization, and the migration of rural people to the cities, more gratifying changes will take place in the urban-rural structure of the population and the industrial structure of rural labor, and the disintegration of the peasantry will be accelerated. As a result, the proportion of traditional farmers, the proportion of the rural population and the proportion of agricultural labor will drop, while the proportion of modern farmers, the proportion of the urban population and the proportion of non-agricultural labor will rise. The transfer of more farmers from farming to other trades and the urbanization of their life style will become new and crucial factors imperceptibly affecting the birth policy of peasant families. In brief, we should let more farmers come into the market economy and let the market economy remold the farmers.

The disintegration of the peasantry will result in old concepts about births fading away and new concepts taking their place. Different counter policies should be taken for different targets. Compulsory control will be necessary in some cases, but for others, services alone and necessary management will be sufficient. Moreover, even if the same policy is applied, the degree or force should be different. Therefore, a new question of "exercising control and management and providing services at different levels" is raised.

Second, raising the market price of work time and increasing the opportunity cost of births.

Under the conditions of a market economy, the most important commodities are perhaps labor and work time. The development of the market economy will lead to the rise of market prices. Where there is acute competition, there is a great shortage of time resources. This is a regular phenomenon. There is no doubt that as work time becomes more expensive, the cost for birth will be greater. That is, more time will be spent on work, study, training and social activities. Therefore, how to allocate the work time and the after-work time (including the time for procreating and bringing up children) in the best way will become a question that must be taken into consideration in the family birth policy.

It is specially worth noting that China has always encouraged young rural women to get involved in non-agricultural businesses and raise the market price of their work time. This has indirectly affected a change in their birth concept and behavior. The rise of the cost of the opportunity for births gives an impetus to the rise of the cost of bringing up children. More births bring a heavy price that they cannot bear. From the long-term point of view, the emancipation of women will be of great importance for the formation of a mechanism for self-restraining the growth of the family size.

Third, including education and training to stimulate the human capital investment of families, especially the increase of the cost of bringing up children.

The modern economy is becoming knowledge-based. It makes greater, higher and new demands on the quality of the workers. More and more people have become aware of the absolute necessity of health, education and training to the competition for survival. There is reason to believe that the health, intelligence and education industries will form a new quaternary industry. This change may produce two results: One, the question of the self-worth of parents will become more outstanding. Two, the proportion of the investment in the family's human capital will rise. Once the growth of a family's income exceeds a given point, the elasticity of the human capital investment to the income growth will be greater. All this will finally help the younger generation of farmers change their own and their children's values, from the pursuit of the low-level demand for food and clothing to the pursuit of a high-quality lifestyle, and from the pursuit of the quantity of children to that of the quality of children.

Since the early 1990s, the reconstruction of the population control mechanism has been characterized mainly by the cultivation of the restraint mechanism of the market economy affecting population growth. The crucial point is the modernization of the birth concept. It should be said that the healthy development of the market economy and the modernization of the birth concept form a process of intergrowth.

From the long-term point of view, the operation of the market economy will undoubtedly be helpful for reducing the birth rate and the completion of the change to a modern population. The great force of the market economy will gradually change the mechanism for the reduction of the birth rate from the compulsory type to the voluntary type. This will be demonstrated microcosmically in the formation of the mechanism for self-restraining the growth of the family. For example, the "Southern Jiangsu Model" on the change to the modern population mode proposed by demographers in 1992 shows that developed areas like southern Jiangsu Province have already begun such a historic shift.[24] Population work will also shift its two strategic focuses at an appropriate time: the shift from the pure control of the quantitative growth of the population to the guarantee of quality of births and the improvement of the quality of the population, and the gradual shift of the function of the administrative departments from population control to exercising management and providing services.

At present, China is in the special historic period of replacing the old system with the new. The spontaneous force that promotes the change to the modern population mode is growing quietly (mainly manifested in the modernization of the birth concept and the formation of the mechanism for self-restraining the family size), but because population control is still in the system environment and historical stage of the initial growth of the market economy, in order to keep the birth rate declining or maintain the status quo with a view to avoiding a disturbing "rebound", it is still necessary to depend on the existing compulsory measures and the increase of the inductive force (publicity, education and services) for population control. Therefore, the historical function of the administrative mechanism for population control should be fully affirmed and improved in the new situation. It is very important to continue to raise the incomes of family planning workers and improve their social image so as to give full play to their enthusiasm and creativeness.

(2) Low Birth Rate: What Course to Follow?

Since the beginning of the 1970s, China's birth rate has

dropped dramatically. By the 1990s, China had become one of the countries with low birth rates. In fact, China had already approached the low birth rate goal in the 1980s.[25] In the 1990s, the total birth rate dropped further, in some places to under the replacement level. Therefore, the judgment that low birth rate has become a reality in China has been accepted by more and more specialists and scholars.

The emergence of the low birth rate presents two important challenges:

1) To persist in family planning despite the low birth rate

The low birth rate in China has its own characteristics.

First, it has been achieved in a not very stable situation. In other words, the current phenomenon of "the birth rate lower than the replacement level" may be temporary. In the initial stage of the market economy, fluctuation and rebound of the birth rate are possible. People must realize soberly that the socio-economic and cultural conditions for the maintenance of a stable low birth rate in China are not adequate.

Second, there are differences or imbalances in the fall of the birth rate among the different regions, different ethnic groups and different strata. Considering these differences and imbalances, it perhaps can be said that China as a whole has not yet fully achieved an all-round and sustained low birth rate, which may be limited to the provinces and municipalities directly under the Central Government.[26] At the same time, regional differences in the change of the birth rate also reflect the differences of the various strata of the population. For example, the birth rate of the urban population, the non-agricultural population and the highly educated population has dropped much more rapidly than that of the rural population, the agricultural population and the less-educated population. These differences and imbalances show that the overall pattern of an all-round and sustained low birth rate has not yet emerged.

Third, while the country has initially achieved the goal of a low birth rate, it also faces a challenge from the momentum of population growth, i.e., the phenomenon of "low birth rate but high increment" people have often talked about. Studies show that the momentum of population growth in China will last 35 years (2000-2035). The momentum of population growth is unavoidable; and the absolute fall of the birth rate is insufficient to solve the problem. The fundamental way to get out of the population dilemma is to deepen the reform and accelerate social and economic development. But the steady reduction in the number of births year by year is also an important aspect of the solution to the population problem.

To alleviate the pressure of the population size, China faces challenges from many other sides, including the problem of the aged population. To reduce the pressure of population growth by paying a cost in other aspects was not the original intention, but people had to come to the conclusion that population growth is the most important part of the population problem and the principal aspect of the contradiction. Moreover, people can create conditions and seize the right time to reduce the price they have to pay in other aspects. In short, in order to alleviate the pressure of the population size, China will continue to strive for an all-round, steady and sustained fall of the birth rate (specifically, to keep the birth rate below the replacement level, and finally return to the replacement level).

2) Under the condition of low fertility rate, China not only should lose no time in conducting family planning, but even more importantly, should do the work well.

Spurred by the serious population situation, people have

raised the new demand to "lose no time in doing the work and doing it well." This is fully understandable. China's population control goal has been achieved through population planning and the implementation of the quotas level by level. The achievement of this goal has often depended on forceful administrative measures. The population control system with quotas makes family planning in China an unusually tough policy, but it has resulted in a low frequency of births. How should we proceed from here? Should we strive for a still lower rate every year? If so, how should we proceed in areas where the plan has been fulfilled 100 percent?

Doing the job well means that, in the present situation, people should switch the approach from management to service, or from stressing quantity of service to stressing quality of service, and from emphasis on the number of births to the improvement of healthy births. To improve the quality of family planning work (such as enhancing the service consciousness and guaranteeing healthy births) can enhance people's consciousness of family planning, thus making it easier to fulfill the targets.

In this connection, we have already set forth the proposition "Seeing the Chinese population problem in a new light" under the new historical conditions, and have held preliminary discussions.[27] In practice, however, we need to adjust our line of thought, eliminate and prevent short-sighted actions, in an effort to solve a whole series of issues.

(3) Out of the "Low-level Equilibrium Trap" of Population Growth

We know that modern economists in the West used to

sum up Thomas Malthus' population theory as the "low-level equilibrium trap" or "Malthusian population trap". More than 200 years ago, Malthus wrote his famous book *An Essay on the Principle of Population*, in which he constructed a theoretical model on the relation between population growth and economic development, which was built on the basis of many very simple suppositions and presumptions. The model has three major suppositions: One, that population growth is laissez-faire and free from interference; two, that the supply of the means of livelihood is limited in a given period; and three, that the returns from land decrease progressively. Based on these suppositions, Malthus concluded that sustained population growth would throw people into the "low-level equilibrium trap" some day. Logical inference and the historical facts we have observed since the time of Malthus show that if there is no force of social change and economic development to draw it forward — or under the supposition that the productive forces are kept in a relatively static state, it seems to be a really unavoidable fact that excessive population growth does indeed lead to the "low-level equilibrium trap". It is obvious, however, that the Malthusian theory bore the brand of his times, and was a concept on the population problem connected with traditional agricultural society.

As many commentators have pointed out, Malthus ignored or did not take into consideration the huge impact of technological advance. Optimistic scholars usually hold that this impact is enough to offset the negative effect of the rapid growth of the population. The growth of the modern economy has been very closely linked with technological advances in the form of scientific inventions, technical innovations and social changes. Increasing, not diminishing, returns of scale have become an outstanding characteristic of the growth of the modern economy.[28] In times entirely different from the past, the phenomenon of population growth leading to low-level equilibrium has become rarer and rarer. Rapid and sustained technological advances have made it possible for all countries and regions to escape from the dark shadow of the Malthusian "population trap". This can be confirmed by the facts of the improvement of the per-capita income, and other indices of the living standard and quality of life in the course of population growth.

Since the beginning of the reform and opening up period in China some twenty years ago, while the Chinese population has been growing by an annual net increase of 14 to 16 million, the economic growth rate has been high and sustained, and the per-capita income has also been increasing. At the same time, the living standard of the people has been notably raised and the quality of life has been further improved.

The relationship between supply and demand in the Chinese market has changed from that of a seller's market to a buyer's market. The living standard of the Chinese people has experienced a historic leap — from having only adequate food and clothing to leading a well-off life. Their centuries-old dream of having no worries about food and clothing has become a reality. This is manifested mainly as follows: First, the incomes of both urban and rural residents have risen by big margins. From 1990 to 2001, the per-capita net income of rural residents rose by 62 percent, and the per-capita disposable income of urban residents more than doubled. The balance of the bank deposits of both urban and rural residents was a little more than 500 billion yuan in 1989, but it had risen to 8,700 billion yuan in 2002. The per-capita disposable income of urban residents was over 7,000 yuan, and the annual per-capita net income of rural residents was 2,500 yuan in 2002. Second, the consumption level and the quality of life have notably improved, and the total consumption has increased year by year. The total retail sales of social consumer goods in China in 2001 increased 4.5 times as compared with 1990. At the same time, a major change has taken place in the structure of consumption. The proportion of the per-capita spending of families on food to their total spending on consumption (the Engel coefficient) dropped from 54.2 percent in 1990 to 37.9 percent in 2001 in urban areas, and from 58.8 percent to 47.7 percent in rural areas. There is no doubt that it is the reform and opening up program as well as sustainable social and economic development that have helped China out of the "low-level equilibrium trap".

Another indication that the Chinese people have begun to get out of the "low-level equilibrium trap" is the great achievements made in the struggle against poverty. It is the common wish of mankind to eliminate poverty, and it has been the consistent policy of the Chinese government to eliminate absolute poverty. It is estimated that the absolutely pauperized population accounted for 60 percent to 70 percent of the total population in old China.[29] After several decades of efforts since the founding of New China, especially after the rapid growth of the economy since the reform and opening up policies were introduced, the living standard of the Chinese people has markedly improved. The absolutely pauperized population dropped from 250 million in the early years of the reform and opening up drive to 65 million in 1995. The absolutely pauperized population in rural areas further dropped to 28.2 million by the end of 2002. The drastic drop of the absolutely pauperized population in China has an important effect on the reduction of poverty worldwide: The pauperized population in China accounted for 28.2 percent of the total pauperized population in the developing countries in 1990, and it dropped to 17.8 percent in 1998. During this period, the pauperized population in the developing countries not including China dropped by 77.5 million, while that in China dropped by 150 million. China's rate of contribution to the world's poverty reduction was as high as 190 percent. James D. Wolfensohn, president of the World Bank, said that the drastic drop in the absolutely pauperized population in China in the past twenty years was a contribution to global poverty reduction bigger than that of any other country. This is a universally acknowledged historical achievement. There is no doubt that the effective system innovation and the sustained economic growth have offset all negative effects from the population growth. It shows that a realistic solution to the population problem can only be found in the process of social and economic development under given historical conditions.

The strong economic growth and the notable social progress in China since the beginning of the reform and opening up drive have lifted large numbers of poverty-stricken people out of the "low-level equilibrium trap". This is an achievement unprecedented in the history of China.

The reform and opening up policies have made a huge contribution to and opened the road for alleviating and solving the population problem in modern China. Of course, we never deny the necessity of losing no time in doing family planning work and doing it well, and making further progress in the new historical period. On the contrary, we hold that family planning and population control are still urgently necessary today, when the low fertility rate goal has been achieved in different parts of China one after another. More-over, the low or high fertility rate itself does not truly reflect the seriousness and extent of the population problem. Fur-thermore, the low fertility rate at present is not stable, but unbalanced and incomplete.[30] Moreover, it can also be said that in the fundamental sense, whether it is necessary to in-troduce planned birth or control the population growth depends, in essence, on the value judgment of policymakers on whether systematic operation completed by the popula-tion, socio-economic and resource environments in the course of their interaction and integration can achieve the goal of coordinated and sustained development as a whole. In this sense, the theoretical basis for population control in China can be regarded as a "theory of coordinated develop-ment" and "theory of sustained development".[31]

To sustainable development in China, population growth is both a challenge and an opportunity. However, the future China will not experience any crisis arising from irresistible population growth. The fundamental state policy of reform and opening up has helped us out of the "low-level equilib-rium trap" and pulled us further away from this trap. China, as the largest developing country in the world and a country which is working hard to build socialism with Chinese char-acteristics, will support the UN's global proposal for the elimination of poverty with a clear attitude, firm confidence and effective measures. It will shoulder its responsibility to eliminate poverty and make its due contribution.

Chapter 4

The Achievement of a Low Fertility Rate and New Problems

Since the beginning of the reform and opening up era, the Chinese birth rate dropped from 33.43 percent in 1970 to 12.86 per thousand in 2002. The number of births in 2002 came to 16.47 million. The human mortality rate has remained 6 to 7 per thousand since 1970. It was 6.41 per thousand in 2002, and the number of deaths was 8.21 million. The natural growth rate of the population dropped from 2.58 percent in 1970 to 6.45 per thousand in 2002. The total fertility rate dropped from 5.81 in 1970 to 1.6-1.8 at present under the replacement level[1]. As a whole, the urban population in China has basically effected the change to the modern population reproduction type with low birth rate, low mortality rate and low growth rate; the rural population is still in the process of this change.[32] Although there is still a dispute on what a low fertility rate is,[33] it is an indisputable fact that the fertility rate in China has dropped drastically, and to a

---

[1] The total fertility rate ≤ 2.5 is generally regarded internationally as a boundary mark for the progress of the population to the low-fertility-rate stage. The total fertility rate of the Chinese population was 2.31 in 1990. A sample survey conducted by the State Family Planning Commission in 1992 among 380,000 people showed that the total fertility rate was 1.7. In its report submitted to the International Population and Development Conference in Cairo in September 1994, the Chinese government confirmed that the Chinese total fertility rate was 2.0. It is now 1.6-1.8. The numerical values are still under dispute, but more and more people are accepting the fact of a "low fertility rate".

fairly low level. Two questions have arisen from this: How could China, as a large economically underdeveloped agricultural country, achieve the goal of low fertility rate in a short period of time? Do the aged population and other problems mean that the change of the fertility rate is inevitably accompanied by the reshaping of the population problem? These two questions are to be discussed in this chapter.

(1) Why Has the Chinese Fertility Rate Dropped so Quickly?

The factors for the rapid drop of the Chinese fertility rate fall into three categories: One, social and economic factors; two, structural or systematic factors; and three, family planning. The drop of the Chinese fertility rate has been achieved within a powerful system framework. Of these factors, the social and economic ones have all along played the basic role. Although the family planning factor is more direct, it has not played the fundamental role. We use the following simple diagram to illustrate the relations between the three categories of variables as outlined above and the fertility rate variable.

Diagram 4-1 Explanation of the Rapid Fall of the Chinese Fertility Rate

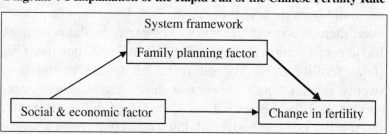

The rapid fall of the Chinese fertility rate is often attributed to the single factor of the population policy. It is true that the effect of the family planning program has been very powerful. But in the final analysis, the effect of the implementation of the family planning program or the effect of the implementation of the population policy was achieved in the given system framework and under the given conditions for social and economic development. In contrast, social and economic factors not only directly affect the birth demand of the people and the birth policy through the effect of the non-planned birth factors such as the social role and role consciousness of the people, but also indirectly affect the change of the fertility rate through restrictions on the objective conditions needed by the acts of planned birth. In any case, the role of the social and economic factors is basic, and this basic role is not only manifested in the restriction on the specific conditions for planned birth placed by social and economic factors and the effect of the execution of the policy, but also in the important effect produced on the change of the fertility rate when family planning is not practiced. Some specific explanations follow:

First, let's look at the social and economic factors. Historical experience shows that the fertility rate drops with social and economic development. So far as the macro relationship between the fertility rate and the income is concerned, they are roughly in inverse proportions (see Diagram 4-2). However, there is a major exception. For example, the per-capita income in China was only US $310 in 1982, but the TFR (total fertility rate) dropped from 7.5 to 2.3 in the next twenty years. China's experience shows that it is not necessary to wait for the natural but slow fall of the fertility rate; the fertility rate can be forced down quickly through a vigorous family planning program.

Diagram 4-2 The Relationship Between Fertility Rate and Income: the Situation in Some of the Developing Countries of East Asia in 1972 and 1982

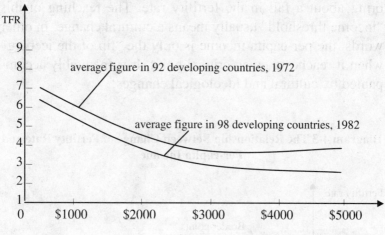

Per-capita income (calculated in US $) in 1980

(Source of data: *1984 Development Report*, p. 177)

From the long-term point of view, the bigger income one has, the fewer children one wants. In other words, people who have more wealth and a better life tend to have fewer children. Homologous to the famous proposition that "poverty produces population", we can, in fact, put forward a proposition that "wealth reduces fertility".

However, it must be noted that it is not high income itself, but the change in people's life brought about by the high income that forces down the fertility rate. This is the first point.

Second, the relationship between the income and the fertility rate varies because of the absolute amounts of income are different (see Diagram 4-3). If the income is below a given critical point, the growth of income will lead to a rise in the fertility rate. Going a step further, if the income is above a given "boundary", the progressive increase of income will bring about a fall in the fertility rate. The reaching of this "income threshold" usually means a cultural change. In other words, the per-capita income is only the "tip of the iceberg" when it reaches a given critical point. It is inevitably accompanied by cultural and ideological changes.

Diagram 4-3 The Relationship Between Change of Fertility Rate and Per-capita Income

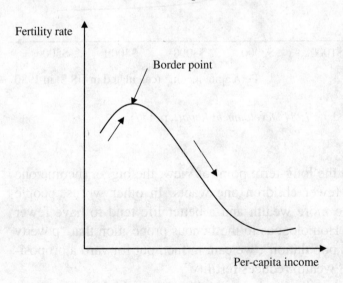

(Source of data: *1984 Development Report*, p. 109)

Comparatively speaking, however, the fall of the fertility rate is even more closely related to the development of education and medical services, as well as poverty reduction. Some studies have shown that the relationship between the fall of the birth rate and the rise of the literacy rate of adults and life expectancy is even closer than that with the macro per-capita GNP. Better education for women is one of the crucial factors in the fall of the fertility rate, because better education for women may, first, be beneficial to late marriage, and, second, be beneficial to the increased efficiency of contraception, thus improving the birth control rate and reducing the fertility rate. Better education may also give women better employment opportunities, and equip them to better look after both themselves and their children.

The initial impetus for the fall of the fertility rate in China has come from social and economic development. The reform and opening up policies have created good social and economic environments for the further fall of the fertility rate. The logic of the fall of the fertility rate caused by the social and economic development is theoretically clear: Economic development, rise of per-capita income, improvement of the quality of the life, change of the traditional ideas, stress on self-worth, attaching importance to the quality instead of quantity of children, family planning, healthy birth and good care of children have become the conscious orientation of action day by day. In other words, economic development has given rise to a self-restraint mechanism for controlling the population through a series of medium variables, and macrocosmically facilitated the fall of the fertility rate and the gradual completion of the change to the modern population mode.

Second, from the system point of view, there have been

unique conditions for the fall of the fertility rate in China.[34] For example, since the founding of the People's Republic, China has attached great importance to educating the people in collectivism, and the idea of the collective and social interests being above everything else has penetrated their minds. Furthermore, frequent legal and ethical education has made it easier for the government to obtain understanding and support from the public for its long-term policies in the interests of the nation. Although the contradiction between state policy and some sections of the public on the birth issue has always existed and even become acute at certain times, persistent education in collectivism has finally integrated the aspirations of the public with the overall goal of the development of society. For another example, the establishment of the socialist system has greatly raised the political and economic position of women. The census conducted in 1982 showed that the employment rate of women in China was higher than in any other country. It is a general law that the fertility rate of employed women is lower than that of housewives without jobs. The social system in China guarantees equality between men and women in education and employment, and in participating in and discussing state affairs, and equal pay for equal work between men and women. This undoubtedly is beneficial to the fall of the fertility rate.

Moreover, since the founding of the People's Republic, several patriotic health campaigns have been launched in both cities and the countryside, a free medical service system has been instituted in the urban areas, and a cooperative medical service system has been instituted in rural areas. All this has greatly helped to reduce the crude mortality rate, and the infant mortality rate in particular, thus creating conditions for the initial fall of the crude birth rate in the late 1960s and 1970s. Historically speaking, the spontaneous fall of the fertility rate is, first of all, because of the fall of the mortality rate (the infant mortality rate in particular). Once the mortality rate falls, the fertility rate will eventually respond to it, and begin to tend to fall.

Finally, the tight administrative system from top to bottom in China has provided the powerful organizational conditions for the mobilization of social resources. In order to promote the large-scale family planning movement, it is essential to concentrate a considerable amount of manpower, materials and finances, and integrate them, and the Chinese administrative system precisely accords with the demand. The above superficial analysis at least shows that the rapid fall of the Chinese fertility rate was accomplished in the given system framework. This is indeed a very unique and important point.

Third, from the angle of family planning, China has accumulated very successful and rich experiences. In fact, the Chinese government began to support and promote family planning activities in the developed regions as early as in the 1950s. Since the 1970s, it has promoted the family planning program forcefully throughout the country, encouraging late marriage, late birth, fewer births and the procreation of healthy babies. Along with economic development, a network for giving publicity to and education on family planning and providing good health services has been improved, and has played a positive role in controlling population growth and improving the quality of the population. Since the end of the 1980s, it has raised the slogan of "losing no time and doing family planning work well," paid attention to the quality of the family planning work, established a systematic population perspective, found a way to combine rural family planning work with the building of a socialist market economy, with the farmers' desire to seek prosperity through honest labor for a well-off life, and with the building of well-cultured and happy small families, achieving great success. In the 1990s, the work pattern for planned birth has been gradually changed to providing health services for reproduction along with economic development.

In concrete practice, two effective principles have been worked out for Chinese family planning work: One, the principle of combining government guidance with people's voluntary actions and giving guidance to different categories in different ways; and two, the principle of placing emphasis on publicity, education, contraception and regular work.

The main content of the Chinese current family planning policy is to encourage late marriage, late birth, and fewer but healthier babies, and encourage couples to have only one child each. Couples in rural areas with real difficulties are permitted to have another child after an interval of a few years. Ethnic minority groups must also practice family planning, and the specific requirements and measures are decided by the governments of the autonomous regions and provinces with sizeable ethnic minority groups. All provinces, autonomous regions and municipalities directly under the Central Government should make corresponding policies and regulations, and formulate their respective local laws and regulations through legal procedures in accordance with state policy and in light of local conditions.[35]

The above analysis shows that the rapid fall of the Chinese fertility rate is not a historical coincidence, but an inevitable outcome of many historical conditions.

(2) Views on the Current Low Fertility Rate in China

China became one of the countries with a low fertility rate as early as in the early 1990s. The development of the Chinese population has shown a new situation. How will the prospects for low and negative growth of the population change? What will be the consequences of the new situation of population growth? How can we explain it theoretically? How should we view the new population phenomenon of low fertility? For China, which has been long troubled by heavy population pressure, low fertility has been a policy goal of the government for a long time. However, a number of new population problems have cropped up one after another, together with the arrival of a period of low fertility.[36] They call for great foresight and vigilance.

At present, different people have different views on the "low fertility" phenomenon. Some people hold that the present fertility rate is adequate, and it is perhaps necessary to make an adjustment to the birth policy (even if only in some local areas); others hold that the low fertility rate at present is only a superficial phenomenon. Because the Chinese mechanism for the fall of the fertility rate is mainly of the compulsory type (especially in the rural areas), the possibility of a rebound of the fertility rate cannot be ruled out. Therefore, even if viewed only from the angle of the relative figures (the fertility rate and growth rate), the problem of the quantity of the population may not necessarily have been solved completely. Also, others hold that China will be troubled by the contradiction of "low fertility rate and high increment" in the foreseeable future, and although the fertility level is low the population situation allows for no optimism. The annual number of newborns is expected to be around 9.6 million-10 million. Therefore, in the 1990s, Peng Peiyun, then state councilor and minister of the State Family Planning Commission, stressed the necessity of fostering the idea of "absolute population figure".[37] Other discussions centered around the consequences of the low fertility rate. The main views are: One, there are both favorable and unfavorable consequences of the sustained low fertility rate; two, the consequences in a general sense can be divided into direct demographic consequences and indirect social and economic consequences; and three, some of the consequences are universal and common. The aged population as an inevitable consequence of the low fertility rate is evidently universal; it is not exclusive to some countries and regions, but an inevitable trend of the global population change.

China's planned birth is different from family planning in other countries.[38] China has a macro development goal, that is, the inclusion of the birth activities of families in the state plans and the network of social management. It should be pointed out, however, that the goal of Chinese population control is not simply the fewer births the better nor the lower the fertility rate the better.[39] To get an understanding of the phenomenon and problem of the low fertility rate not only helps to do the family planning work well and promptly in the new situation, it also helps us to see the population problem in a new light and to tackle it in a comprehensive way.

There are two categories of population problems: One, the primary population problems caused by the variables of the population statistics, and two, the social and economic consequences caused by the many changes of the population trend, also called secondary population problems. Of course, the primary problems and the secondary problems are interwoven in most cases.

So far as China is concerned, the attainment of the low fertility rate goal is something heartening, as it shows that the country has made very great successes in controlling the population, thus greatly helping to restrain the third human birth peak and alleviate future population pressure. However, as mentioned above, fewer births do not mean a perfect solution. We will tackle the new problems and new challenges arising from the low fertility rate as soon as possible. And we must keep sober-minded on this matter.

So far as our present knowledge is concerned, the modern static population with a zero growth rate is a global trend and aim. However, the developed industrialized countries and the late-developing countries have traversed different roads. In the former, the zero growth of the population and the attainment of the replacement level for the fertility rate emerged almost at the same time. It is quite a different picture in the developing countries. It will still take a period of time to shift from the low fertility rate to zero growth. Related studies have pointed out that this period of time should cover roughly half a century in China, and even longer in India, Western Asia and Africa. This will cause big differ-ences in the change of the population growth in different countries. In developing countries, where the population trend changes faster, from the beginning of the change of the mortality rate to the attainment of zero growth, the size of the population will increase about three times. China is one of these countries. In most countries, the population will increase about five times or even more than six times. This is likely to happen in some countries in Africa, and West and South Asia. On the other hand, this period of time will at the same time provide an opportunity for future policy choices.

Chinese scholars once believed that in order to avoid the fall of the fertility rate from causing too serious a problem in respect to the relative growth of the aged population, it could be adjusted through a family planning policy.[40] Man has great ability to regulate his own birth behavior. But it should be pointed out that the best regulation of the fertility rate is ahead-of-time and orderly regulation. It would be too late to regulate the fertility rate when the disadvantages of the low fertility rate (of course there are also many advantages) are fully revealed. Moreover, the birth behavior of man is by no means entirely controllable. Objectively, birth is uncontrollable. Especially when the modern birth culture characterized by "fewer births, late births, healthy births and even no births" once takes shape, it will exert a strong impact on the birth desire and birth behavior of people, and at the same time become a momentum of population growth.

How should we view the low fertility rate phenomenon in China at present?

First of all, it can be asserted that China has already become one of the countries with a low fertility rate, up to the international standards. The total fertility rate of Chinese women was 2.29, still above the replacement level, in 1990. It began to drop below the replacement level in 1991. Since the early 1990s, the proportion of Chinese women bearing children after the age of 35 has been very small. Therefore, the average number of births by women up to the age of 35 can basically represent the lifetime fertility rate of the women in the year of the investigation. The lifetime fertility rate in the nation was 1.81, or 1.98 in rural areas and 1.22 in urban areas in 2001. Since 1990, the Chinese fertility level as a whole has tended to drop in a steady way. The total fertility rate dropped from 2.29 in 1990 to 1.8 in 2001. The birth rate and natural growth rate dropped from 21.06 per thousand and 14.39 per thousand, respectively, in 1990 to 13.38 per thousand and 6.95 per thousand, respectively, in 2001. As is well known, China's total fertility rate dropped, with fluctuations, in the early and mid-1980s, and has dropped further since the beginning of the 1990s. However, the population change and the social and economic changes have been very rapid in recent years, and are interwoven. Therefore, the fall of the fertility rate in the early 1990s was bewildering, and demographers have found it difficult to determine the degree of the effects of various factors (such as family planning work, social and economic development). However, it is certain that in the latter period of the change to the modern population, the impact of "development" has become important.

Second, the fall of the Chinese fertility rate has been one of the rapidest in the world — comparable with that of Japan. However, the achievement of the low fertility rate in China has its particularity. It is related to the Eastern pattern of population change, which is different from that in the West. The population change in China was effected by relying on massive efforts to practice planned birth at a time when the level of its social and economic development was not high. If we differentiate the patterns of population change into the spontaneous type and induced type, China's is undoubtedly the latter.[41] In the course of the fall of the fertility rate, the effect of planned birth lies in guiding and accelerating the change of the population, but the results of the implementation of the population policy are predicated on social and economic development, and are conditioned by social and economic development. If the amelioration of the Chinese population situation is to be completed, it is necessary to prevent the rebound of the fertility rate in the period of the initial growth of the market economy on the one hand, and to make positive efforts to strive for the favorable effects of modernization on population change on the other.

Third, it is important to pay attention to the difference between town and country as well as regional differences in the change of the fertility rate. Since great efforts have been made to practice birth control, the dual urban and rural birth pattern has always been an objective reality. From the 1970s to the end of the 1990s, the basic pattern of the fertility rate in different parts of the country has not undergone a fundamental change. In most of the vast Chinese rural areas, there are many couples each with two children.

From what has been said above, we can come to the conclusion that although China has become one of the countries with a low fertility rate, and most experts at present believe that China's total fertility rate is between 1.6 and 1.8 and is continuing to drop to below the replacement level, the task of the change of the fertility rate is still far from being fulfilled. China is still confronted with the arduous mission of effecting the second and third changes in the fertility rate (keeping it under the replacement level and finally returning it to the replacement level) in the early years of the 21st century.

Finally, we would like to stress again that the advent of the low fertility age and the reality of the change to the modern population standard do not at all mean that a fundamental solution to the population problem has been found.

(3) New Problems Arising from the Low Birth Rate

First of all, we would like to explain that the "consequences of low fertility" dealt with hereafter are neutral in the original sense — they can be either good consequences or bad consequences. The good consequences of low fertility have been discussed by scholars in detail.[42] In simple terms, it has essentially relieved the pressure of the population growth and created a relatively good population environment and conditions for the modernization of the social economy.

Then, what are the new population problems as the direct negative consequences of the low fertility rate? We think that it is still too early to make an accurate judgment on this. This is because: 1) The consequences of the low fertility rate are wide and overlapping. If we say that the direct consequence is in the demographic sense, the indirect consequence contains rich social and economic implications. In most cases, these are closely interrelated. 2) As the patterns and methods for the population change are different, and national and regional conditions vary, there are surely different manifestations of the consequences of the low fertility rate between the developed industrialized countries and the late-developing countries. 3) There are both general consequences and particular consequences of the low fertility rate. The general consequences are the aged population, the increasing age of the old people, the old age of the labor force and the relative shortage of young and middle-aged workers. The particular consequences include the one-child problem.

In light of the actual conditions in developed countries and in China, the following problems accompanying sustained low fertility merit attention:

1) The problem of low fertility and stable population growth

Low fertility is usually measured by the standard of virtually reaching the replacement level, the net reproduction rate of one in the more accurate terms of population statistics. Considering the mortality rate in China, the total fertility rate of 2.1 to 2.2 is often used as the replacement level. In all the present developing countries, because population growth reaches the replacement level after a period of change, population growth will not stop immediately (or reach zero growth). As to how long it will take to reach zero growth, it is a question that warrants study. Whether to achieve it quickly, at a moderate speed or slowly involves the intensity of the momentum of population growth and the expectations when zero growth is achieved. In essence, the speed of reduction of the fertility rate should take into consideration the necessity and possibility of setting a population goal and ensuring the attainment of the goal. Moreover, it is essential to consider that the policy decision to stabilize the population size, and reduce or slow down the population growth must also be made in advance after the zero growth of the population is achieved so as to avoid "abrupt stop" or "acceleration".

2) The problem of the aging of the population and the aged population

The aging of the population is an inevitable outcome of the change to the modern population standard, but the low fertility rate has given rise to the aging of the population after a given period of time. The aging of the population and the low fertility rate do not occur simultaneously. There are many consequences of the low fertility rate, but the core of the matter is the aging of the population and the aged population. Studies on the relations between the low fertility rate and the aging of the population have received great attention from the government and all walks of life in China.

We hold that the aging of the population involves a structural problem. What is really important is the problem of the increasing age of the old people.[43] The aged people inevitably demand more social security and services. This is the first point. Second, the aged society is a society that needs ethics more than others. We must not only give aged people material support, but also pay great attention to their "spiritual support" problem. This is a universal social responsibility and moral requirement for a healthy aged society. Third, together with the sustained low fertility rate and the rapid aging of the population, the problems of health, reemployment and re-socialization will become more acute. On the one hand, an aged healthy population will become the common pursuit of mankind in the 21st century, and "health" will be one of the primary and basic prerequisites for solving the problems of the aged population. On the other hand, aging of the population will, in a way, lead to an acute crisis of human resources, and the development of the aged human resources will become a focal point in the development of overall human resources. The question of the continued employment and reemployment of aged people is now being put on the agendas of governments at all levels.

3) The problem of the shortage of labor

At the same time as the fertility rate falls, China also faces the difficult problem of the employment of labor. In the foreseeable future, the quantitative supply of labor being greater than demand and the qualitative supply of labor being short of the demand will be a hard problem that China will have to make great efforts to solve. Generally speaking, China is extremely short of high-quality labor required to meet the needs of rapid social and economic development. It should be seen, however, that the emergence of the labor employment peak and the low fertility rate are only phenomena of associated growth. There is no inevitable relation of cause and effect between them. From the demographic angle, the arrival of the employment peak is an effect of the cyclic copy of the active labor born in the previous baby boom, and is caused by the momentum of development of the age structure of the population.

However, accompanying the sustained low fertility rate, the shortage of labor in the demographic sense at any given time is indeed a general consequence of the low fertility rate. The conditions in China are fairly special and complicated. Although the aging of the labor force is an inevitable trend and has already started to become apparent, surplus labor as a whole is, after all, a principal contradiction. Moreover, the shortage of labor in the demographic sense (a type of reduced supply) will not be as serious as in the developed countries in the foreseeable future. It should be specially pointed out that what China is short of is not ordinary human resources (ordinary labor), but special human resources (highly trained and educated people).[44] Therefore, China will not alleviate its shortage of labor through the policy of encouraging births, as the developed industrialized countries do, but attach importance to: 1) balancing the allocation of human resources among the regions through migration, and 2) paying attention to the development and utilization of the aged human resources (especially educated people).

There is one thing in particular that has aroused attention. That is, in the countries and regions where the goal of a low fertility rate has been achieved, a major policy issue is that of retraining the labor force. In order to meet the demands of competition, high technology and developed education are necessary to the growth of a modern economy. The issue of the quality of labor has been put high on the agenda for the first time. In China, the problem of the low quality of labor has existed for a long time, but it is not caused by the low fertility rate. However, the attainment of the goal of the low fertility rate has begun to make the problem of the quality of the labor more outstanding, because a shortage of labor in the demographic sense makes the improvement of the quality of labor (namely, the strategy of "quality replacing quantity") all the more necessary to ensure the attainment of economic goals. In southern Jiangsu region, when the change to the modern population mode was effected, emphasis of population work has been put on the improvement of the quality of the population to meet the needs of economic development, such as promoting good prenatal and postnatal health care, providing vocational and technical education and training.

From what has been said above, we can draw the conclusion that if the attainment of the goal of a low fertility rate fails to give rise to an economic takeoff, it will not be possible to solve the new population problems arising from the sustained low fertility rate in a satisfactory way. This is because, as indicated above, from the angle of the cause of the problem, the new population problems are more or less, directly or indirectly, related to the fall of the fertility rate. But from the angle of the solution, the adjustment of the fertility rate is not the best policy. We should attach more importance to social and economic development, the redistribution of the population, and the deepening of the reforms in the urban and rural areas.

4) The "only child" problem

So far as China is concerned, the new population problems arising from the low fertility rate also include the problem of the "only child". This is a complicated sociological problem. In the narrow sense, the so-called problem of

the only child refers to the problem of the individual character and conduct of a good number of only sons and only
daughters; or in explicit terms, it is a problem of inappropri-
ate education for the only children. However, in the broad
sense, the only child problem also includes at least: one, the
problem of conflicts among different generations in some of
the single-child families, giving rise to an impassable "generation gap". Two, the future problem of support for the aged
in single-child families. The problem of the "four, two, one"
family composition (referring to one child, two parents and
four aged people (two paternal grand parents and two mater-
nal grand parents) is now only a theoretical presumption, but
the problem of providing support for the parents of the single
child is an objective reality in the future, and the problem of
providing support is not only embodied in the material pro-
visions (we should see that the give and take between parents
and children in many Chinese families are imbalanced or
even reversed), but also in the sphere of spiritual support.
Three, there is also the problem of the marriage of the only
child. The quality of their marriages and families can hardly
be guaranteed because of their own limitations, and may
even cause damage to the quality (social order and social
customs) of society itself. All this merits discussion and
study in theory and hard work in practice. It should be
pointed out, however, that the social problems of single children have indeed appeared, but they are not inevitable, nor
can they be attributed to "one birth". They can be well
solved through family and school education, and by creating
a good social environment.

5) The gender ratio problem

The high ratio of newborn males to newborn females
from the early 1980s onward has aroused wide concern at

home and abroad. As a matter of fact, this is not a problem in Chinese cities, where couples have no partiality for either male or female babies. This is related to their educational quality and their better-off life. In Chinese rural areas, the government has given more publicity to the problem, and the old idea of showing partiality for male babies has also been changed considerably. There is every reason to believe that the problem of an imbalanced gender ratio will not last long.

Chapter 5

Migration of Farmers and China's Reform and Development

The migration of Chinese farmers[1] from rural areas to cities has attracted great attention both at home and abroad in recent years. The large-scale migration of farmers is an inevitable historical process in the early period of an economic takeoff. It is precisely the migration of farmers that has impacted the social and economic pattern of separated administrations in town and country, but a new pattern for the harmonious development of the town and country is gradually taking shape in different parts of the country.

The migration of farmers has produced many visible positive effects, which are taking an absolutely predominant

---

[1] The targets we are going to discuss in this chapter are defined as "migrating farmers", not "flowing farmers". This is based on the consideration that the Chinese farmers today are undergoing a great change, involving change of jobs, residences and status. The farming communities that have cultivated farmlands from generation to generation have begun to disintegrate because of this change. The new generation of farmers is becoming urbanized, their residences have changed in quality, and many have become an actual part of the urban population. Their production, consumption and other activities have already been included in the operational system of the overall urban civilization. Their mentality and behavior have also changed considerably. It is too superficial to regard them as farmers merely on the basis of their "registered residences". Therefore, the groups we are discussing in this chapter include both the farmers who have not yet changed their residences (from country to town) and those who have already changed their residences. To combine the subjects into one, we have called this "migration of farmers".

place. For example, it has helped farming families in less-developed areas to shake off poverty and achieve prosperity, helped to relieve the employment pressure of surplus rural labor, and helped to develop tertiary industry in the cities. Broadly speaking, it has helped establish the basic framework of the market economy — the optimum allocation of human resources through the market mechanism, and helped promote the modernization of the nation as a whole. The migration of farmers looking for work in cities has also caused some problems: For example, it has aggravated the crime rate, increased pressure on infrastructure facilities in the cities and produced an adverse effect on environmental sanitation and the general appearance of cities. At present, educational circles and the government have virtually reached a common consensus on the trans-regional migration of farmers: From the strategic angle of long-term development, the unprecedented migration of farmers has more advantages than disadvantages. With the gradual perfection of the market economy system, migration of farmers will move gradually from disorder to good order, and from partial order to full order. In policy orientation, there should be more persuasion used than compulsory measures.

Moreover, the problems mentioned above can be regarded either as problems caused by the migration of farmers or as the outcome of the change of the old institutional structure lagging behind the pace of reshaping the social, economic and population structures. It can be asserted that most of the problems caused by the migration of farmers are problems arising from social transformation and economic development and problems arising in the course of the change from the old pattern of separate administration of town and country to coordinated integration.

(1) Migration of Farmers Seeking Work in Cities

"The tide of farmers seeking work in cities" can be regarded both as an outcome of the reform and a booster for the reform. The household contract responsibility system with remuneration linked to output, the mushrooming of rural enterprises and the rapid progress in the urbanization of the rural population can be regarded as three big steps taken in the sequential development of the reform in Chinese rural areas. China in the new century is facing a still deeper and broader social change, and one of the boosters for this change is the migration of farmers looking for work in cities as its main manifestation.

The trans-regional migration of farmers (from countryside to towns or from less-developed provinces to developed provinces) is a historical tide spurred by the dual action of the market mechanism and macro control. It is, in fact, a process of optimization of the dynamic allocation of the essential factors of production, namely, a process of the transfer of rural labor from sectors and areas with low marginal labor productivity and marginal returns to sectors and areas with high marginal labor productivity and marginal returns. The tide of farmers seeking work in cities today is different from the flood of refugees in the past history of China, when famines, wars and pestilences forced huge crowds of farmers to leave their land. The migration today is a considered act of the farmers who, each with his or her own plot of farmland, are seeking a better life and maximum income after shaking off poverty and having enough food and clothing.

In the modern history of China, the "problem of refugees" was a manifestation of domestic troubles and foreign invasions under the historical conditions of the old times. It persisted, too, into the early years of the founding of New China in 1949. At that time, the system of separate administration for the urban and rural areas had not yet been established. Therefore, large amounts of rural surplus labor flowed into cities, causing many problems.[45] Starting in the late 1950s, with the establishment and consolidation of the residence registration system, the food grain and cooking oil rationing system and the people's commune system, the free migration of farmers from country to town was stopped. Over a fairly long period, farmers could only leave their farms by joining the army, being recruited into factories or other organizations as workers, or passing entrance exams for higher education. But, in fact, the number of farmers who could do so was very limited, and there was no longer the minimum structural environment for large-scale free migration.[46] This produced extremely grave consequences. On the one hand, the weak agricultural economic system had to bear the pressure of the growing consumption demand (for food in particular) and employment demand of the huge population. Relative poverty and even absolute poverty were common everywhere. On the other hand, agriculture provided a large amount of funds for industrialization in cities, but this provided few jobs for the farmers, who found it difficult to receive any monetary income.

In other words, the emergence of "the tide of farmers seeking work in cities" had deep roots in the long-time dual structure of the urban and rural economies. China once adopted a powerful structural restriction and system screen to prevent the rural population from sharing the benefits of industrialization. As a result, the urbanization of the rural population lagged behind. According to the World Bank's

World Development Report of 1985, the level of urbanization in China in the 1980s was not only far below that in developed countries, but even below the average level in low-income countries. China has paid a high price for this, especially in its failure to absorb surplus rural labor into the cities at an adequate rate.

The Chinese nation has made a solid stride forward on the road of seeking common prosperity since the beginning of the reform and opening period. However, not only do the economic gap and the problem of comparative interests among different regions and between town and country in China still exist, but the induction from the "differentials of comparative interests" arising from the gap in the macro aspect among the regions and between the towns and the countryside has been the motive force for the "tide of the farmers seeking work in cities." In the 1960s, U.S. scholar Everett S. Lee advanced a systematic theory of population migration, or the "push-pull" theory.[47] For the first time in history, he defined the factors affecting internal migration and classified them into the two categories of "push factors" and "pull factors". He regarded the former as negative factors, because they urged migrants (or refugees) to leave their original residences. The latter were regarded as positive factors, because they attracted migrants with the desire to improve their livelihood to migrate (or drift) into new residences. In fact, however, there were factors which were both positive and negative (and even "fuzzy variables", on whose value it was difficult to pass judgment) in both the places they migrate from and in the places they migrate to. In concrete terms, in the places from which they migrate, apart from the "push" factors, there are also "gravitation" factors at the same time. Therefore, the net effect of the push factors must exclude the effect of the "gravitation" factors. Likewise, to the potential migrating population, there are also "repulsion" factors apart from the "pull" factors in their target destinations. Therefore, the net effect of the pull factors must also exclude the effect of the "repulsion" factors.

The "tide of farmers seeking work in cities" can also be explained by the push-pull theory.

First of all, the general consensus is that the migration of farmers to urban areas in most cases is caused by push factors. The shortage of farmland merits attention, but it is only a superficial phenomenon. In fact, as illustrated in Guangdong Province, even if the per-capita farmland resources are the same, there is also the problem of differences in labor productivity and marginal returns. The substantial push factor is the shortage of opportunities for development. Of course, all this is closely related to population pressure. Employment pressure is severe almost everywhere in China's rural areas. The rural labor that must be transferred or is willing to be transferred totals at least 100 million people.

Also, low-income returns from agriculture drives farmers to seek work in cities. In this sense, it can be said that this phenomenon reflects the problem of the livelihood of the farmers in the dual structure of the urban and rural economies, the problem of agricultural returns and the problem of the development of the rural areas.

Second, about the pulling factors. As we have observed, the tide of farmers seeking work in cities is mainly a movement of surplus labor from the less-developed regions in the hinterland to the Pearl River Delta, the Yangtze River Delta, Beijing, Tianjin and other developed coastal areas. From the angle of a macro analysis, to the peasant workers, the most important and most realistic pull factors are job opportunities and higher incomes. Job-hunting farmers are classified into the following categories:

One, those organized by local governments. The laborers are under control, have clear objectives, and are given jobs as soon as they arrive at their destinations.

Two, those who get jobs mainly through relatives who have preceded them, and have found work in urban areas. This form of migration helps to avoid recklessness in the search for jobs and is a widespread and important channel of employment in China at present.

Three, a small number of peasant laborers with no help either from governments or relatives seek casual jobs in cities during slack farming seasons. Those who fail to find jobs become part of the rootless floating population.

This blind influx is a major factor causing social instability. Farmers who drift into cities and fail to find work are worse off than they were in their own villages.

China has already carried out a series of reforms to facilitate the flow of the essential factors of production and rationalize the allocation of resources, so as to further liberate and develop the productive forces in the new structure of coordinated development in urban and rural areas.

The reform measures roughly include: 1) Control over the prices of food grains and cooking oil has been relaxed, and the rationing of means of livelihood has been abolished, so that peasant laborers find no difficulty in obtaining means of subsistence. They no longer meet any system barriers, but have market support. 2) The establishment of the identity card system has greatly reduced the function of the residence registration system. 3) The innovative system for the transfer of land-use rights has straightened out relations for the transfer of rural labor, making it possible for farmers to be away from their farmland and even from home. The so-called system for the transfer of land-use rights means that the farmers are permitted to rent and transfer their land-use rights through the market mechanism. According to the report on the establishment of the system for the transfer of land-use rights in Luliang Prefecture, Shanxi Province, farmers sublease their contracted land to people with the ability to cultivate it, not only avoiding the problem of leaving the land uncultivated, and protecting the land resources so that the land resources become important targets for investment and the scale management of land is realized, but also freeing the farmers from their worries so that they can engage in non-agricultural production without fear. Thus it has given rise to a new economic growth point of great significance and with a bright future: agricultural stock cooperative enterprises with farmland as their targets for development. At the same time, the system for the transfer of land-use rights has made it possible for guest farmers to contract farmland. While the local farmers go to factories or cities as workers or do businesses away from home, farmers from outside come to contract their farmland and engage in scaled management. It may well be said that each has a stake in this.[48] The new form of contracting farmland through the transfer of land-use rights has received a positive response from both local and guest farmers. It has become a desirable form of and an important link in the transfer of rural labor.[49]

(2) Non-agricultural Work and Urbanization: an Important Direction for China's Modernization

The key to China's modernization is the modernization

of the farmers (the movement of farmers to other trades, urbanization and better education for farmers), the modernization of agriculture (the extensive use of scientific knowledge and technologies, mechanization and better protection of the ecological environment) and the modernization of the rural areas (industrialization of the rural structure, urbanization of the social formation and integration of the urban and rural structures). The question concerning the tide of farmers seeking work in cities is not whether it is "orderly" or "disorderly", but whether they will be "urbanized" in the modern sense, and become an important force in the coordinated development of the urban and rural economies while more and more farmers engage in other trades.

First, a major problem China faces in the course of its modernization is to turn the employment pressure of the surplus labor into a motive force for its social and economic development. There are many positive effects of the "tide of farmers seeking work in cities." Its most conspicuous macro effect is to have created a new space for survival and development for the huge rural population, effectively reduced the employment pressure in the vast rural areas, shifted the population burden into population wealth, turned disadvantages into advantages, and developed the abundant human resources in the countryside in a rational way. Second, the emergence of the "tide of farmers seeking work in cities" shows that the transfer of rural labor in China has entered a new historical phase — from the phase of internal transfer mainly with farmers "leaving farmland but doing other jobs at home" to the phase of external transfer, mainly with farmers "leaving both farmland and home," or in other words, from "local transfer" to "trans-regional transfer", and from "transfer of farmers to other trades" to "urbanization". This great social change has an extremely profound significance. It shows that Chinese farmers who have depended on farmland for a living since time immemorial have begun to involve themselves in the magnificent process of modernization, and share the social and economic returns from this.

Labor export requires little investment, but produces quick and good results. It has become a "pillar industry" in promoting the rural economy, a new economic growth point and an important measure to develop the economy and make people prosperous. It not only helps to transfer surplus labor and lessen the employment pressure, but also brings funds, technology and information into the countryside.

Third, apart from helping their home villages and themselves shake off poverty and become prosperous, migrant farming laborers have also created huge wealth for society and made contributions to China's economic takeoff.

Fourth, the emergence of the "tide of farmers seeking work in cities" has helped to train large numbers of talented people, increased the ability of the farmers to adapt themselves to the market economy, broadened their field of vision, and renewed their concepts, thus creating technical, managerial and psychological conditions for the development of non-agricultural businesses in less-developed regions. By going to coastal cities to work or do business, large numbers of former farmers have learned advanced skills, and returned home to develop their local economies.

In short, the contributions made by these farmers can be summed up as follows: They helped to alleviate the employment pressure (or optimize the allocation of labor resources), increase their incomes, promote economic construction and improve their own quality. The reform and opening up program, and the building of a market economy require the participation of the whole nation. History will draw the farmers to the market and temper them in the rising waves of the market economy, and give them a new lease of life. The resultant material, cultural and spiritual prosperity is not only a blessing for the farmers themselves, but also a major symbol of the successes achieved in the era of China's reform and opening up.

Moreover, the Chinese government attaches great importance to the problem of ensuring the proper and orderly movement of farming laborers. From the angle of the coordinated development of urban and rural areas, the two are interrelated.

(3) "Revitalizing the Population" and Achieving Social Stability

The current migration of farmers essentially echoes the transformation of the society, economic changes and the reconstruction of a new urban-rural structure. It is by migrating to shake off poverty and attain prosperity that Chinese farmers have attained a new mental outlook and proven themselves to be an important aspect of the modernization of the country.

The separation of town from country has historically led to the impoverishment of the rural population. In this sense, what constitutes the greatest threat to social stability in China is the mixture of poverty and unemployment. It is true that the migration of farmers has involved some negative factors that might lead to instability, but if the farmers were not permitted to change their living conditions through migration, and were compelled to be haunted by the contradiction of more people and less farmland, if the separate administration for the urban and rural areas could not be replaced by coordinated development in urban and rural areas, if large numbers of surplus laborers stayed idle in rural areas and were left out of the process of modernization, they would constitute a deep root cause of overall instability. To increase the income of the farmers and to provide them with more jobs is crucial to stability not only in rural areas but also in China as a whole. To stabilize the farmers, it is first of all necessary to develop agriculture, encourage the farmers to cultivate their farmland intensively and extensively, establish more rural enterprises to absorb part of the surplus rural labor through rural development, and to gradually reduce the unlimited supply of surplus labor by tightening the birth-control policy. Although the tide of farmers seeking work in cities cannot solve the problem fundamentally, more and more facts have shown that proper and planned migration of farmers may well be accepted as a good channel to achieve rural stability.

As a strategic consideration, China not only does not try to halt the tide, but on the contrary it has created conditions to open up more space (space for employment, space for survival and space for development) for the transfer of rural labor to urban areas, including the building of towns by farmers themselves.

To sum up, we have come to the following conclusions:

1) The emergence of the "tide of farmers seeking work in cities" in the late 1980s and 1990s was historically inevitable, realistic and rational. It was an irresistible trend. The tide was, in essence, a transfer of farmers to other trades, but it was also in a sense a reflection of the demand of the Chinese farmers for urbanization and their participation in it. It has

had a profound significance for China's modernization.

2) The in-depth problems revealed in the course of migration were not the problems of transport, growth of cities and crimes, but the problems of farmers, agriculture and rural areas. In the narrow sense, they are the problems of employment, income and circumstances of the farmers. In the broad sense, they are the problems of the comparative interests of agriculture, the opportunities for rural development, and also the problem of coordinated development in urban and rural areas.

3) Seeking both temporary and permanent solutions to these problems. On the one hand, it is necessary to weaken the outward push from rural areas, and on the other, to increase the demand pull from target areas, so as to solve the problem of the oversupply of rural labor. For example, the Ministry of Agriculture has stressed the need to develop rural areas and agriculture (such as by means of diversified economy and township enterprises) and reduce the push as much as possible. It also emphasizes that rural labor should be absorbed mainly in rural areas.

4) From the angle of weakening the push, it is necessary to attach importance to the problem of the livelihood of the farmers and the problem of rural development from the high plane of strategy. At present, the support given by the developed regions in the east to the west in funds, technology and talented people is significant. Among the outstanding examples, the famous Huaxi Village in Jiangsu Province has helped some poor inland areas train managerial and technical personnel for the development of township enterprises. Some specialists and scholars believe that to improve the environment for investment in the central and western parts of China is crucial to the development of township enterprises in these

regions and an important measure to weaken the migration push in the less-developed regions. Experiences from various areas have shown that to support agriculture with industry, to feed agriculture with part of the industrial income, to combine agriculture, industry and commerce, to combine agriculture, science and education, and to combine crop growing, animal husbandry and the processing industry are good ways to develop agriculture and rural areas as a whole. It is essential to guarantee the legitimate rights and interests of the farmers, not only in policy but also in law. At present, to improve the conditions for the subsistence of the farmers and further straighten out the relations between town and country and between industry and agriculture will help to reduce the negative effect of the tide of migration.

5) From the angle of providing more jobs, sustained economic growth in the coastal regions will continue to demand more peasant laborers. Besides, the development of non-agricultural industrial zones and the construction of more small towns as well as the growth of large urban areas are of great significance for the transfer of rural labor from the long-term point of view.

6) In order to ensure the transfer of rural labor in a proper and orderly way, it is very important to cultivate relatively unified multi-level labor markets and labor cooperation relations on both the regional and national levels. From the national angle, the "Orderly Trans-regional Transfer of Rural Labor — First Phase of the Project of the Coordinated Employment Program for Urban and Rural Areas" issued by the Ministry of Labor is a step in the right direction.

7) At the same time, it is still a strategic measure to control the number of births and slow down the growth of rural labor. Of course, attention should be paid to the combination

of family planning work with extra efforts to aid the poor regions.

8) We should promote compulsory education in an earnest way, strengthen rural professional training work, and raise overall competitiveness supported by quality so as to meet the demand for social and economic development in the urban and rural areas. As pointed out above, the biggest barrier to the transfer of rural labor is its low educational and technical quality, and even its low all-round cultural level. We should attach special importance to this.

9) The shortage of railway and road transport facilities during given times (such as the Spring Festival and other long holidays) is now being tackled, so as to facilitate the movement of farmers.

Chapter 6

The Problem of the Quality of the Chinese Population

While the idea of "controlling the quantity of the population" has long been appreciated by the nation as a whole, the idea of "improving the quality of the population" is also being gradually fostered. The current situation of the quality of the Chinese population is not satisfactory. The proportion of illiterates at and above the age of 15 in China to the total population dropped from 33.58 per cent in 1964, when the second census was conducted (the illiterate population counted in 1964 included all those who had never learned to read and write at and above the age of 13), to 22.81 percent at the time of the third census in 1982, and further to 15.88 percent at the time of the fourth census in 1990. It was 6.72 percent at the time of the fifth census in 2000, but the absolute number was still as high as 85.07 million.

More and more people with broad vision have become strongly aware that to improve the quality of the current working population and the new generation of workers is an important point of penetration to turn the pressure of the population into the dynamism of the population and turn its unfavorable situation into a favorable one.

The improvement of the quality of the population is of profound significance. First, the quality as a "potential energy" means the growth of potential forces of production, and its development is crucial to the growth of the modern economy. Second, the quality of the population is an important component part of the overall national strength. Third, the quality of the population is a scarce and special "resource", with the characteristics of activity and multiplication. Fourth, for China, the improvement of the quality of the population is also a requisite for increasing and consolidating the effect of population control. The improvement of the educational quality of women in particular is a crucial factor in getting them to bear fewer children. The improvement of the quality of the population is even an important prerequisite for doing away with the historical approval of high fertility.

(1) What Is "the Quality of the Population"?

As is well known, concern for the problem of the quality of the population is a salient feature of population studies in China. More and more people with broad vision are reaching a consensus that the ultimate purpose of population control is to improve the quality of the nation and raise the standard of life.

As a matter of fact, "the quality of the population" has always been an inseparable part of population studies in China. As early as in the 1930s, Chen Da, one of the pioneers of modern population studies in China, proposed the necessity of "improving the quality of the population" by giving birth to healthy babies and providing education.[50] In the 1950s, Ma Yinchu wrote in his famous *New Population Theory*: "The quantity and the quality of the population in our country do not match each other." He also said, "It is essential to make great efforts to improve the quality of the population, and raise the health and educational levels of mankind."[51] Since the 1980s, with the deepening of the reform and opening-up efforts, demographic studies, which had been silent for many years, flourished again, and made great progress in a short time. Concomitantly, research into the "problem of the quality of the population" was developed on an unprecedented scale.

The quality of the population is a comprehensive category reflecting the prescribed quality of the total population in a given time and space, and is a universal generalization and summary of the prescribed quality of the population in many aspects. It is reflected in the conditions and ability of the total population to know and change the world.[52] In brief, it is a combination of physical strength and intellectual power. On the basis of the simplest and the most essential prescriptions, we have divided, in this book, the extensions of population quality into three factors — physical quality, intellectual quality and non-intellectual quality (the latter two can also be called "psychological quality" in a broad sense).[53] More concretely, physical quality refers to physiological health, such as physical strength and stamina. The psychological factor directly involved in the process of cognition is the intellectual factor, and the psychological factor not directly involved in the process of cognition is the non-intellectual factor. The intellectual quality consists of the basic abilities, such as the power of observation, faculty of memory, mental power, imaginative power and operational power. The non-intellectual quality includes the kinetic energy element and the composite element. The kinetic energy element consists of demand, emotion, motive and attention, and the composite element is composed of will, temperament, esthetic sense and appreciation of social life. If the physical qualities reflect the stamina of the population, the psychological qualities reflect its intellectual power. In this sense, the physical qualities (or physiological qualities) and the psychological qualities are characteristics of the external manifestation of the latent energy of the quality of the population (see Diagram 6-1).

Diagram 6-1 Structural Explanation and Analysis of the Quality of the Population

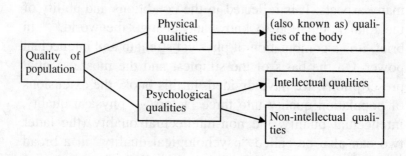

(2) Enlightenment from "the Phenomenon of the Water Bucket": a Supposition of the Population Quality Theory

If a wooden bucket has an uneven brim, with some of the boards making up the sides shorter than others, it is obvious that if the water in the bucket is in excess of the shortest board, the water will spill over automatically. In other words, the amount of water contained in the bucket is determined not by the longest board, but by the shortest. Therefore, if the capacity of the bucket is to be increased, the only way is to replace the shortest board with a longer one.

From this illustration, we can envisage a basic "population quality water bucket" theory: Under given historical conditions, the limit to the potential of the quality of a certain population group is controlled by the shortest "board", namely, the weakest aspect of the quality. Here, we can liken the "amount of water" contained in the bucket to the potential of the quality of the population; and the three "boards" that make up the "quality bucket" are the "physical quality board", the "intellectual quality board" or the "educational quality board", and the "non-intellectual quality board" or the "psychological quality board" (in the narrow sense).

The "short quality board" always exists objectively, and is constantly changing. It may be the physical quality, the educational quality or the psychological quality. We have realized that when the "short board of the quality" is fixed, the advantages of the long and medium boards of the quality are only potential, and can hardly be exploited. This is the "limit effect of the shortest board".

On the basis of this "theory of the population quality bucket", we have come to realize that if the potential of the quality of human resources is to be exploited to the maximum, apart from giving full play to its advantages, it is essential to pay attention to the "limiting effect of the shortest board" at all times and weaken its impeding effect by making the short board longer, so as to better tap the potential of the population quality.

From the angle of the individuals who make up a population group, this theory is also true. For example, if a person with extraordinary natural gifts and a strong character has poor physical quality, it is quite possible for his superb talent and boundless fighting spirit to be annihilated because of his physical fragility. On the other hand, if a person is physically strong and very clever, but his fighting spirit is not strong, his personal character is not firm and his habits are bad, it is also fully possible for him to accomplish nothing. With regard to both a social group and an individual person, the "limiting effect of the shortest board" should not be neglected.

It is obvious that the level of potential quality is exactly the level limited by the index of the short board, or in other words, the level of potential quality is not determined by the advantages, but by the disadvantage of a person, i.e., the shortest "board". Therefore, it is extremely important to find the disadvantage, and weaken the "limiting effect of the shortest board". There is no doubt that the potential quality equals the product of the area of the bottom of the quality bucket (representing the congenial organism quality or the hereditary quality) multiplied by the index of the short board of the quality bucket. It can be seen that if the level is to be increased continually to approach the expected level, it is essential to continually weaken the "effect of the short board" through the purposeful investment of human capital.

The returns from the investment of human capital are directly related to which "population board" the investment is made in. Therefore, it is far from enough to stop at "making an appeal for the quick improvement of the quality of the Chinese population". Neither is it enough to be aware that "the higher the quality of the population the better". Here we have taken into consideration the inherent structural relations of the quality, made an accurate judgment of the quality of which aspect should be improved first, and given the "right prescription for the illness" so as to achieve twice the result

100

with half the effort. In brief, in accordance with the "theory of the population quality bucket", we can achieve the best returns only by investing in the shortest population board. It can be said that this conclusion has enriched the current knowledge of the theory of human capital. We could call this practice the investment strategy of "lengthening the short board" and weakening the "limiting effect of the short board" to raise the quality and development levels of the population.

It is not easy to decide which is the "shortest board" of the quality of the Chinese population. From the angle of the relations between the population and the country's economic development, available studies hold[54] that the quality level of the Chinese population is ahead of the level of the country's economic development. This judgment is based on the fact that when the per-capita GNP in China is lower than the world average, the life quality index of the Chinese population (PQLI) is higher than the world average.

It must be pointed out, however, that PQLI as an indicator for measuring the life quality proposed in the West in the early 1970s can only reflect the good or bad physical and educational qualities of the population groups relatively, but cannot reflect the strong or weak non-intellectual psychological quality of the population groups. This is the first point. Second, there is a striking contrast between China's geographic economy and social development. Therefore, the thesis that "the level of the quality of the Chinese population is ahead of the level of the country's economic development" has failed to face the fact of regional differences. Moreover, it is also difficult to reflect the educational quality of the modern population in an overall way by using only the single indicator of the adult literacy rate. In short, the inference that "the current quality level of the Chinese population is ahead of the level of the country's economic development" by calculating and comparing the PQLI values is tenable only in a relative sense.

The high or low quality of the population can only be a relative judgment, but in the absolute sense, the value of improving the quality of the population to the social and economic development is doubtless — "the higher the better".

The current quality of the Chinese population is, in form, compatible with the country's social and economic development, but it is incompatible in structure. Although the current physical and intellectual qualities of the people are compatible with the country's social and economic development, or even ahead of the latter, the population's non-intellectual quality is incompatible with China's social and economic development.

The "non-intellectual quality" of the Chinese population is the "shortest population board", thus restricting the physical and intellectual quality potential of the population. This also more or less explains the contradiction between the rational judgment that "the quality of the Chinese population is ahead of the level of the country's social and economic development" and the perceptual knowledge that "it is difficult for the current quality of the Chinese population to meet the requirements of modernization." The two parallel phenomena show that the physical and intellectual qualities of the Chinese population contain an abundance of latent energy waiting to be fully, effectively and rationally developed and utilized. The most urgent thing at present is to accurately discover or diagnose the "shortest population board" and lengthen it through the investment of human capital to overcome the "short board effect".

(3) Making Efforts to Increase the "Gold Content" of Human Resources

Population is one of the leading variables affecting the process of development. To make an economic analysis of the population issue is one of the most basic and most important aspects of the work of social scientists. It is very important to look at the population problem, the employment problem, the consumption problem and the distribution problem from the angle of economics, but if we want to link these problems and find out the economic intension of the Chinese population fundamentally, perhaps we cannot but start from the angle of "resources". As is well known, from the angle of medium-term and long-term development, most of the resources of the mankind (whether natural or social) are scarce. As a matter of fact, since the middle of the 20th century, mankind has universally acknowledged that "the shortage of resources" has become a global issue and one of the primary "bottlenecks" in the course of sustainable development of the mankind. An important task of modern economics is to study how to allocate and utilize scare resources more economically under given historical conditions. The modern concept of "resources" has broad implications. All the conditions needed for the development of social health can, in a sense, be regarded as "resources". So far as modern economic growth is concerned, human resources, capital resources, natural resources, information resources and time resources are the five major basic resources. Among them, the human resources (especially resources of talented people) are the most important form of social and economic resources. Successful economic growth rates recorded at home and abroad have shown that the quality of human resources has become a factor of growing importance to economic output. Thereupon, a new concept of development was evolved — that is, using the development of the mankind itself to promote and guarantee sustainable social and economic development.

From the angle of the development of resources, population resources take three forms, which make up a pyramidal structure owning to their inherent correlations, as shown in Diagram 6-2.

Diagram 6-2 The Three Forms of Population Resources

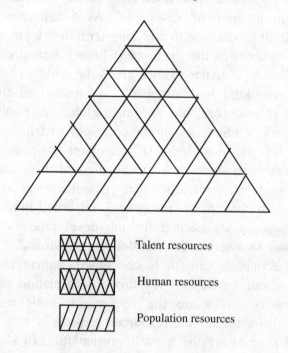

Talent resources

Human resources

Population resources

The population resources in the figure refer to the total population, but do not include the "zero quality population" whose quality index is zero and therefore has no resource value.

The so-called human resources refer, in fact, to all population resources with working ability, but generally to adult labor resources (people over the age of 15). Retired people with the possibility of reemployment are also included in the category of human resources. Of course, the main body of human resources is the population of working age (between 15 and 64 years).

Talent resources refer to the working population with special skills. In modern society, there is no lack of self-taught talented people, but the growth of the majority of the talent resources is inseparable from a given amount of human investment.

According to the pyramidal composition of population resources, if human resources constitute a bigger percentage of the population resources, it shows that the resources are abundant, but these are only ordinary resources, like ordinary mineral deposits. If the talent resources account for a bigger percentage of the population resources, this also shows that the resources are plentiful. But these are special resources with special value. They are the "gold and silver deposits" in the population resources, and entail good prospects for development. If the talent resources account for a higher percentage of the human resources, it shows that the human resources have a high "gold" content, and they are fine-quality human resources.

Apparently, to judge whether a country has an abundance of human resources, first, one has to look at the high or low proportion of the human resources to the total population resources, and second, at the high or low proportion of the special human resources (namely talent resources) to the total human resources.

If the population resources as a whole are mainly manifested as the existence of a consumption force, ordinary labor resources can seemingly be regarded as the existence of a "human hand" or an operating force. Only the characteristic of the special talent resources is an entity similar to the "human brain", in essence a creative power. Here, the operating force is also a productive force, but it is not high grade; it is only the productive force as a creative power that is high grade.

If "population control" is a kind of regulation of the flow of population — being a function of reducing total demand and thereby weakening and controlling consumption power — then the "use of the human hand" or the "development of the human brain" is a kind of opening up of sources, its function being to liberate and develop the productive forces. Simultaneous attention must be paid to the regulation of the flow and opening up the sources, but the latter undoubtedly plays a bigger role, and is therefore more important. Whether to control the quantity of the population or to improve the quality of the population, the ultimate goal should be the full, effective and rational development of the available human resources, because it is the real source of national wealth, and the true theme of civilization and progress.

We should not pin our eyes only on the "regulation of the flow", but stress the opening up of sources — by using the human hand and developing the human brain to increase the total productive forces. What is particularly important is to make great efforts to develop the brain resources contained in the tens of millions of China's intellectuals.

China has a population of 1.3 billion. In other words, it has 1.3 billion brains. If it can acquire the "brain advantage" of its huge population, by educating hundreds of millions of Chinese to have sound and well-developed brains, and everyone has a proper job and can give full play to his or her talent, there will be no doubt that China will have a prosperous future. This is the reason for and the significance of developing the strategy of rejuvenating the nation through science and education.

The current situation in China is that the ordinary human resources are more than enough, but the special human resources are relatively insufficient.

The quality of the working population in China is not high. The percentage of the highly educated population in China is small, while that of the number of people with less than junior middle school education is large. The population aged 25-64 having received senior secondary and higher education accounted for 18 percent of the total population in 2000, while those with junior middle and lower schooling accounted for 82 percent, and those with primary and even less education constituted 42 percent. In other words, there were only five highly educated people for every 100 Chinese people.

The unavoidable aging of the population will also adversely affect the quantity and quality of the human resources. The aging of the population will cause no shortage of labor resources; on the contrary, we will continue to suffer the pressure of demand for employment. It should be pointed out, however, that this is a purely quantitative viewpoint. If we look at the problem from the angle of economics, sociology and other branches of social science, the actual situation in the future will surely be more complicated than the pure population quantity forecast. For example, the problems of structural and regional shortages of human resources will emerge one after another.

The population resources in China are indeed very abundant, but from the angle of international competition, the human resources that can actually be used are insufficient. To solve this important problem, China attaches importance to making two major changes: One, changing the population resources into qualified human resources through a population quality investment project, and two, changing the ordinary human resources into fine-quality talent resources through a human capital investment project.

The "gold content" in the Chinese population resources is not high. In order to turn the quantitative advantage of the Chinese population resources into an actual economic advantage, the Chinese government attaches great importance to the population quality and human capital investment strategies.

(4) The Rights and Wrongs of the Negative Development of the Population

The topic of the negative development of the population is closely related to the current measures to control the population. It is an objective fact that some of the people in the less-developed regions and rural areas still tend to have more babies, while the people in the developed regions and urban areas have fewer children. Some people worry that if things go on like this, the proportion of the low-quality population will rise. This is the so-called negative development of the population quality.

What exactly is the "negative development of the population"?

There are different answers to this question. The so-called negative development of the population refers to the diminishing proportion of the high-quality population to the total population and the process or phenomenon of the increasing proportion of the low-quality population to the total population.[55] Alternatively, it can refer to the phenomenon of the increasing proportion of the low- and zero-quality population to the total population, giving rise to the evil effect of "survival of the worst".[56] Of course, the so-called high or low quality discussed above is relative.

By retrieving the relevant documents, we have found it easy to discover that when almost all critics have discussed the rights and wrongs of the "negative development" question, they have all based their arguments on the relative differences in the urban and rural fertility rates, and even directly used the urban and rural differences of the fertility rates to reflect the trend and degree of the negative development of the quality of the population. However, there is still much doubt about whether the urban and rural differences in the fertility rate are sufficient to make differences of the quality of the population show up in the future. This kind of supposition is almost a reproduction of the saying "dragons beget dragons, phoenixes beget phoenixes; like father, like son". Naturally, the studies and conclusions based on this kind of supposition are hardly tenable.

First, what is of vital importance to the development of the quality of the population is rather the difference in the process of the social and economic development than the relative changes or differences in the fertility rate. It is true that the rural fertility level is higher than in cities and towns, but this does not mean that the proportion of the rural population will become bigger and bigger. Quite on the contrary,

China is now in the historical period of rapid urbanization of the rural population. As a result of industrialization, the transfer of much rural labor to other trades and urbanization, the percentage of the rural population will surely go down year by year. When the first census was conducted, in 1953, the percentage of the urban population was 13.26 percent. It had risen to 18.3 percent in 1964, when the second census was conducted, to 20.6 percent in 1982, when the third census was conducted, to 26.23 percent in 1990, when the fourth census was conducted, and to 36.09 percent in 2000, when the fifth census was conducted. According to a forecast made by the Chinese Urban Development Report for 2001-2002, issued in December 2002, the urbanization rate in China is expected to rise from 37 percent to more than 75 percent in the next 50 years, ushering in a new historical period of rapid urbanization in China. Therefore, from the dynamic angle, the differences between the urban and rural fertility rate will not be reflected in the proportions of the distributions of the absolute figures of the urban and rural populations.

Second, the supposition that the quality of the urban population is higher than that of the rural population is not indisputable. From the angle of educational quality, it is roughly tenable, but from the angle of the physical quality, it is not so certain. There are not a few people with a long life in the rural areas.

But the question of "negative development" should arouse attention and alertness. The vicious circle of "more babies and inferior babies" may be serious in the relatively closed and under-developed communities. However, from the overall point of view or from the angle of development, "negative development" is nothing to be afraid of.

As is well known, poverty and low quality are closely related. Poverty often means undernourishment and less education. Therefore, the change of the proportion of the poverty-stricken population can roughly reflect the change of the proportion of the inferior-quality population. China's reform and opening that will bring immediate benefits and contribute to future centuries, and its sustained development has put an end to the negative development of the quality of the population in the old days in the circle of "more babies and inferior babies", and reconstructed the positive selection mechanism for the quality of the population, the force of which is becoming stronger.

When discussing "negative development", we should not neglect "positive development". It is better to discuss them together, because the level of development of the quality of the population is inevitably the outcome of the growth or decline of the two forces of positive and negative development, as well as a product of the dynamic balance of the positive and negative social selection mechanisms. But when "negative development" rises to be the main aspect and overtakes "positive development", the problem becomes very serious.

Generally speaking, the high or low quality of a population is determined by the joint action of heredity and environment. The environment here is the "macro environment", which covers the two major systems of natural environment and social environment. And the social environment can also be subdivided into the categories of system environment, policy environment, economic environment, cultural environment, living environment, working environment, and so on. There is still controversy as to which affects the quality of a population more, heredity or environment.

It is true that it is difficult to tell clearly which is minor and which is major on the individual level, heredity or environment, inborn or acquired, and nature or nurture, but the history of the evolution of mankind shows that the environment factor is more important.

So far as the affecting factors are concerned, the negative elimination of the population is possible in a given scope (macro, medium and micro), but it is by no means uncontrollable. The crucial thing is that we take a dynamic and development point of view. What is more important, the environment factor can be changed, and is, in fact, being changed.

As mentioned above, survival of the fittest is predominant throughout the country. Although the vicious circle of having more and inferior-quality babies still exists, more and more couples are having fewer births and healthier babies. Because of the joint action of social and economic development and population control, the vicious circle seen in some areas or populations is giving way to a benign circle. Above all, population control has reduced, not enlarged, the size and scope of the negative development of the population. This can also be regarded as an indirect function of population control in improving the quality of the population.

It can be anticipated that the healthy development of the market economy will improve the social selection mechanism for the survival of the fittest of the Chinese population, and the optimization of the environmental system as a whole will further weaken the effect of "negative development" in some areas. The quality of the population falls into social and historical categories. The trend of development is to constantly improve the quality of the population in less-developed regions. For example, with the rapid transfer of large amounts of rural labor to other trades, and urbanization and the gradual integration of the urban and rural areas, the quality of the new generation of Chinese farmers today is totally different from what it was in the past.

Of course, the whole is made up of parts. In this sense, we should pay attention to the "negative development" phenomenon in some areas. There should be no differences over the preventive measures to be taken in this respect.

Chapter 7

China's Aging Population and Countermeasures

China entered the stage of being an aged society at the turn of the 21st century. A discussion on the effect of this population situation on the long-term development of China will obviously help us get to know the relations between population and sustainable development in an overall, systematic and profound way.

(1) The Current Situation, Trends and Basic Features of China's Aging Population

Population aging is a global trend, and China is no exception. When the fifth census was conducted in 2000, the number of persons aged 65 and over was found to account for 6.96 percent of the total population in China. By another criterion, the number of persons aged 60 and over has surpassed 130 million today. (See the following diagram)

Diagram 7-1 Changes of the Age Proportions of the Chinese Population

1953~2000 (Unit: percent)

Year of census	0-14 yrs	15-16 yrs	65 yrs+
1953	36.28	59.31	4.41
1964	40.69	55.75	3.56
1982	33.59	61.5	4.91
1990	27.69	66.74	5.57
2000	22.89	70.15	6.96

Source: *The Primary Data of the 5th National Census, 2000*, compiled by the Census Office of the State Council and the Population and Social Science and Technology Statistics Department of the State Statistical Bureau, published by China Statistics Publishing House, 2001

If we look further, it is not difficult for us to conclude that the first half of the 21st century will be a period of accelerated aging of the Chinese population. The number of persons aged 60 and over is expected to be 165 million by 2010, 230 million by 2020, and more than 400 million by 2050, the peak period of the aged society. It is worth noting that while the aged population is growing rapidly, the problem of the structural aging of old people is also becoming more and more conspicuous.

In fact, China entered the era of "population aging" very early in some areas. For example, Shanghai became an aged society as early as in 1982, when the third census was conducted. During the Eighth Five-year Plan period (1990-1995), Beijing, Tianjin, Jiangsu and Zhejiang crossed the threshold of the "aged society". From the angle of development, the four provinces of Shandong, Guangdong, Liaoning and Sichuan also entered the "aged society" one after another during the Ninth Five-year Plan period (1995-2000).

These developments have shown that the trend toward an aged population in China first appeared in 1982, and the tendency has become stronger and stronger in the subsequent years. By 2020, the aged society will emerge in almost all parts of the country.[57] In the face of the rapid aging of the population, we must take positive measures to cope with the resulting circumstances and challenges.

The aged population in China has two major characteristics.

One, the speed of aging of the Chinese population may be the fastest in the world. This is because the total fertility rate has dropped very rapidly, and at the same time life expectancy has been lengthened. In the 1990s, the fertility rate dropped further — to replacement level — about eight years ahead of schedule.[58] It has now dropped to under the replacement level. This means that the Chinese population is aging more rapidly than expected.

Two, aging of the population in China is ahead of the country's social and economic modernization. China has entered the stage of an aged society ahead of time, when its per-capita income is not high and its overall national strength is limited. This forms a striking contrast with the situation in the developed industrialized countries.

The aged society in China has been achieved by quick and artificial methods. While the fertility rate was reduced by big margins, the ill side effects arising from this were unexpected. The problem of the cost of the fall of the fertility rate has begun to attract wide attention.[59] In short, the rapid and ahead-of-time aging of the Chinese population may mean that we are facing the problems of an aged society before we have the corresponding economic strength and social security ability to cope with them. We have realized this, and are taking positive steps in this regard.

(2) Systematic Analysis of the Problems of the Aging Population

The so-called problems of the aging population refer to the ill social effects produced by the operation of the population system — the evolution of the age structure of the population, and its challenge to sustainable economic and social development. In concrete words, the problems arising from the aging population roughly include: the problem of providing social support and medical care for the aged, the problem of the labor shortage in an aging society, the problem of intergeneration relations, and so on. We will deal with these problems one by one.

Generally speaking, social support for the aged includes material support, consolation and care, none of which should be neglected. It should be stressed that social support for the aged should not be regarded as mere material support. The second question is who should provide the support. The first case is "self-support" — good health and guaranteed income (so far as the guaranteed income is concerned, some people receive retirement pensions from the state, and some from state-owned enterprises. In the future, most of them will receive support from social insurance. Some people call social insurance organized by the state or income received directly from the "state social security". In some rural areas, the aged received part of their income from the collective economy). Self-reliance and "savings for old age" are specific forms of self-support. The second case is the "support from children" or "family support" — the aged may live together with their children or separately. This form is more popular at present and will continue to be so for the foreseeable future. It is stressed in the Law on the Protection of the Rights and Interests of the Elderly, this form of support for the aged plays a useful role at the present stage, especially in the rural areas. The third case is "support from relatives". The fourth case is "support from charitable people". These latter two forms often apply to the aged who have no children. The fifth case is "support from society" for people such as widows and widowers or the households of infirm and childless old people. These are usually taken care of by collectives or communities. Another form of "support from society" is free board and lodging in "homes for the aged". We regard the fully-paid board and lodging in homes for the aged as a form of "social services for the aged", and not as a form of "support from society". Today, the support system for the aged with Chinese characteristics consists of four pillars, namely, the state, communities (or collectives), families and individuals. A realistic choice for the future is the simultaneous existence of different forms of support for the aged with local characteristics.

To improve the quality of their lives in their remaining years, aged people must think of how to reserve, control and develop three resources of vital importance: the financial resource of "income", the biological resource of "health" and the social resource of "relations" — including both family relations resources, such as conjugal harmony and filial children, and social relations resources. As the saying goes, "A close neighbor means more than a distant relative". If one has abundant and good quality resources of relations with neighbors, colleagues and friends (harmonious relations and strong inter-personal cohesiveness), it will also help greatly improve the "quality of support" for oneself.

Rapid population aging has made medical security for the aged an outstanding problem that must be solved with priority through medical reform in urban areas and the improvement of the cooperative medical service in rural areas.

This is also true of the problem of social services. On the one hand, the aged groups, as especially weak groups in society, objectively have strong demands for all kinds of social services. On the other hand, the income of the aged has made it difficult to develop the paid social services as desired. "Volunteer services" should be encouraged. Such services at present are virtually free of charge. This practice may play an unexpected role in promoting cultural and ideological progress. It can be seen that if "volunteer service" becomes a common practice and is passed on from generation to generation, the "volunteers" themselves may, as a matter of fact, also receive services from the next generation of volunteers when they become old. This kind of service is maintained mainly by raising the ethical standards of the members of society.

The problem of shortage of labor in an aged society is still not a pressing one in China, but it will crop up sooner or later, particularly in the areas where the aging of the population began sooner and there is a higher proportion of aged people.

An aging society faces a chronic challenge from the continual decline of vigor and vitality. However, the decline is by no means uncontrollable. By ensuring the health of aged people, we can increase the vigor and vitality of the aging society.

Next, there is the problem of intergeneration relations of an aged society. With the advent of an aging population, and with the establishment and perfection of the social security system, the wealth among different generations has begun to be distributed and operated in the entire social system, and intergeneration relations of support are gradually becoming socialized, legalized and standardized. This is good for guaranteeing the quality of the life of the aged, but it is also a challenge for whether the old, young and middle-aged people can live together in harmony in the course of sharing the social wealth.

The problems of old people can be summarized as follows: The elderly are financially supported, medically looked after, meaningfully occupied, culturally updated and recreationally entertained. In addition to the problems of old people, the problems of an aging population also include the problem of the social burden (such as old-age pensions and medical insurance), the problem of social vitality, the problem of labor shortage, and the problem of inter-generational relations.

(3) New Understanding of the "Golden Age Structure"

A view that has been in circulation for a long time is that the total dependency ratio of the Chinese population will show a tendency to fall gradually during the 20 to 30 years from the mid-1990s into the 21st century. This means that the proportion of the population who can participate in economic activities and create social wealth will rise and the number of dependent persons will decrease. The period of the change of the age structure of the population has been called by some scholars the period of the "golden age structure of the population", because of its potential for creating favorable conditions for economic development. In other words, it can be regarded as a positive effect of the change of the age structure of the population in the future. However, this is not entirely accurate.

Dependency ratio is a term used in demography to refer to the populations of children and old people dependent on the population of working age. Generally speaking, there are three categories — total dependency ratio, child dependency ratio and the dependency ratio of old persons. As indicated in the following tables, the dependency ratio of the Chinese population has shown a tendency to fall. Theoretically, the economic implication of the dependency ratio is simple and explicit. It is generally held that the fall of the dependency ratio means less-burdensome dependency on society. It is said that one of the important effects produced by the change of the age structure of the population on economic growth in Japan was that the continual fall of the total dependency ratio in a given period created good population conditions. The city-state of Singapore had a similar historical experience during its stage of economic takeoff. Therefore, demographers regard the period during which the dependency ratio of the population falls or is maintained at a low level as a "golden period" during the change of the age structure of the population.

Diagram 7-2 Changes in the Dependency Ratio of the Chinese Population (1953-1990)

Year	Total dependency ratio (%)		Child dependency ratio (%)		Aged dependency ratio (%)	
	Standard I	Standard II	Standard I	Standard II	Standard I	Standard II
1953	77.30	68.63	64.33	61.21	12.98	7.42
1964	86.88	79.53	75.52	73.07	11.36	6.46
1982	70.39	62.60	57.35	54.63	13.04	7.97
1990	56.72	49.69	43.28	41.35	13.43	8.34

Note: Total dependency ratio = (child population + aged population) / population of work age. Child dependency ratio = child population / population of work age. Aged dependency ratio = aged population / population of work age. The child age here is 0~14. The age of the elderly is divided into two categories: Aged 60 and over (Standard I) and aged 65 and over (Standard II); the age of the population of work age is also divided into two categories: Aged 15~59 (Standard I) and aged 15~64 (Standard II).

Diagram 7-3 International Comparisons of Dependency Ratios (%)

Year	The world	Developed countries	Developing countries	China
Total population dependency ratio				
1950	74.2	64.3	79.5	69.5
1975	83.1	66.7	90.0	86.6
1985	73.0	61.4	77.1	61.6
2000	67.2	64.5	68.0	58.5
2025	64.1	76.4	61.7	59.5
Child population dependency ratio				
1950	60.2	45.6	68.0	56.8
1975	67.5	41.4	78.4	73.6
1985	57.7	35.8	65.4	47.9
2000	50.6	34.3	55.0	42.9
2025	40.7	34.8	41.7	30.0
Aged population dependency ratio				
1950	14.0	18.7	11.5	12.7
1975	15.6	25.3	11.6	13.0
1985	15.3	25.6	11.7	13.2
2000	16.6	30.2	13.0	15.6
2025	23.4	41.6	20.0	29.5

Source: *World Population Prospects, 1990.* For the predicted figures for China, please refer to Du Peng's *A Study of the Process of the Aging Population in China,* published by the Chinese People's University Press, 1994

China's dependency ratio has dropped, as the pressure from the surplus of the population continues. According to a prediction for the change in the absolute numbers, the labor surplus will show a tendency to grow. Second, when discussing the economic implications of the "dependency ratio", we not only see the change of the population factor, but also the complicated effects of the non-population variables. Comparatively speaking, the national conditions in China are rather complicated and atypical. Whether in population conditions, educational background or stage of economic growth, it differs greatly from Japan and Singapore. Furthermore, what we have discussed so far is dependency ratio. In reality, because of the changes of the numerator and denominator, the actual value of the dependency ratio is bound to depart from the theoretical value.

Therefore, we take a prudent attitude toward the argument of "the golden age structure of the population".

We have seen quite clearly that the aging population has become a reality in China with the advent of the 21st century. We regard the aged as wealth, not a burden. We attach importance to investment in the human capital of the aged and the development of their human resources.

At present, the most prominent worry is the rise of the dependency ratio of the aged population and the increased burden they pose for society. However, the demographic definition of the aged population as a purely dependent population does not tally with the facts. In reality, many of the aged are self-supporting, and even support others. Obvi-

123

ously, when more and more seniors in good health are still working after retirement age, the "theoretical dependency ratio" reflects the actual situation less and less accurately. From the difference between the two sets of dependency ratios, we can theorize that, through the development of the aged human resources, more and more older people can be separated from the "dependent population" and become physically fit and even make new contributions to society.

Of course, the first premise for the elderly to be meaningfully occupied is that they have a sound mind and sound body, and keep themselves physically fit and vigorous to prolong their life span. Investment in health pays dividends in the form of staving off dependency among the aged. This "saving for health" activity should start among the young and middle-aged population, and even children.

The arrival of the aging society has increased the importance of developing the human resources of the aged population. Elderly people in good health and with a certain working ability (those with special skills in particular) will become an increasingly important part of the human resources for the development of the country. An analysis of the data obtained during the fifth national census in 2000 shows that of the entire workforce, the number of persons aged 60 and over constituted 6.3 percent. This figure breaks down to 3 percent for those aged 60-64, and 3.3 percent for those aged 65 and over. In addition, 4.6 percent of the employed were aged from 55 to 59. As for reemployment, 50 percent of workers in the 60-64 age group were reemployed, and of those aged 65 and over, 25 percent were reemployed. In total, about 33 percent of all people at or above 60 years were employed.

To sum up, to achieve the sustainable development of society at large, we should never ignore the trend of population aging, but make a correct strategic choice, that is, to include the question of achieving a healthy and productive aged population in the total strategic framework of sustainable development. For this purpose, it is essential to attach great importance to investment in health and savings for health of the aged groups, and pay great attention to "giving meaningful jobs to the elderly". These are the two essential strategic bases for building a healthy aging society.

(4) The Aged: a Burden or Resource?

Facing the challenge of the rapid aging of the population, we have renewed our concept of "human resources". Human resources are no longer regarded as the population of working age in the given age period (from 15 to 60 or 65), but the total number of people with working ability, naturally including more and more elderly people in good health. It can be asserted that the importance of aged human resources is growing with the accelerated process of population aging. Elderly people in good health (those with skills in particular) are wealth, not a burden on the country.

We realize that the knowledge, skills and experience of the elderly in good health as well as their professional dedication and sense of responsibility are priceless assets. The elderly have just as much right as the young and middle-aged to participate in the competition for jobs. Therefore, it is necessary to oppose "age discrimination" in the labor market, and reduce and finally prevent the phenomena of "intergenerational conflict". It is even necessary to adopt preferential policies to guarantee the employment of older people, and set up a special reemployment market for them. In fact, a center to tap the skills of retired people was set up in Beijing as long ago as in 1988.

In short, the reemployment of older people is not only necessary for their subsistence, it is also needed for the development of society. We should give more publicity and encouragement through the media and policies to ensure that older people in good health and with the ability to work have opportunities to do so.

(5) A Permanent Solution: Striving for a Healthy Aged Community

In the past two decades and more, the understanding and practice of "healthy aging" has received wide attention in the developed countries. In China, "healthy aging" has also become the basic strategy for meeting the challenge from population aging, formulated by the China Gerontology Society.

First, a healthy aged society should be efficient and full of vigor. In this sense, "healthy aging" and "productive aging" are two aspects of the same issue. Healthy aging means that while physiological and calendar aging cannot be avoided, older people can keep themselves younger psychologically. Psychological vigor and youthfulness can delay physiological decline. Even physiological aging should be controlled with every effort to make sure that it is normal aging and not pathological aging.

Second, a healthy aging society ensures equal opportunities and equal competition among the different generations. At the same time, the distribution of wealth among the different generations not only fully reflects the principle of to each according to his work, but also reflects the humanitarian spirit of the mankind and the social ideal of seeking common prosperity. Common prosperity should not ignore the aged groups. In addition, old-age pensions should be linked to changes in the cost of living, so that old people will fully enjoy the fruits of economic and social development.

Third, a healthy aged society is one in which income and medical care are guaranteed. Governments at all levels should adopt different strategies for different subgroups of the aged population.

Fourth, a healthy aged society is a society with dignity, with the motto "To care for the elderly is to care for ourselves."

Obviously, "age discrimination", "ability discrimination" etc. all go against this goal. The dignity of old people is embodied not only in the respect for them shown by the younger generations and the security provided by society, but also in their being able to further realize their self-worth. An aged society with dignity must have the backing of a culture with respect for the elderly. This virtue, embedded in Chinese culture for thousands of years, is precious intellectual wealth for building a healthy aged society and is also a priceless cultural heritage of mankind.

It can be said that to build a healthy aging society is not only an obligation in the course of building socialism with Chinese characteristics, it can also be regarded as a common value orientation of the human society in the 21st century. In this way Chinese culture has something unique and precious to contribute.

Finally, a healthy aging society is a society featured by sustainable development. As population aging has become the most outstanding population trend at the beginning of the 21st century, "health aging" and the achievement of "healthy aged society" will inevitably create excellent population conditions for the sustainable development of society at large. Just as healthy aging is a prerequisite for the achievement of a healthy aged society, the achievement of a healthy aged society also constitutes an indispensable and important requisite for the sustainable development of society at large.

We have a well-planned goal, but our task is arduous and the road ahead is long. We are making concerted efforts in the course of the following preparations:

Theoretical preparation: Only by making theoretical preparation in advance, can we act in a farsighted manner.

Publicity preparation: We are giving wide publicity to new population developments through the mass media, so that both the government and the public can become fully aware of the trends and characteristics of the aging population and the challenge we jointly face.

Material preparation: Only through the accumulation of wealth can we achieve the goal of seeking common prosperity and lay the groundwork for socialist reform. In the final analysis, development is the top priority.

Mental preparation: Challenges and opportunities stemming from the aging of society coexist. We face them calmly, but we are fully prepared for any eventuality. We attach great importance to them both strategically and tactically.

System preparation: A healthy aged society can be achieved only under the condition of a perfect rule of law. Support systems needed for a healthy aged society have been studied intensively. The Law on the Protection of the Rights and Interests of the Elderly was adopted at the 21st meeting of the Standing Committee of the 8th National People's

Congress, and went into force on October 1, 1996. This was a very encouraging step.

Personnel preparation: Gerontology will become a well-developed and popular "sunrise branch of science" worldwide in the 21st century. China will be no exception. In order to reveal the law of development related to the aging of individuals and groups, the training of research personnel has been put on the agenda.

Chapter 8

The Chinese Population and Sustainable Development

General-secretary Jiang Zemin stated at the 5th Plenary Session of the 14th Central Committee of the Communist Party of China: "In the course of modernization, we must regard it as a major strategy to realize sustainable development." In his "Explanations on the Drawing up of the Ninth Five-year Plan for National Economic and Social Development and the Proposals for the Prospective Targets for 2010", then Premier Li Peng said, "The Ninth Five-year Plan and the 15-year prospective targets must embody the guiding principle of sustainable development. This will bring benefits to the present generation as well as future generations." It can thus be seen that "sustainable development" is a strategic principle China attaches great importance to. As the embodiment of the government will and at the same time a positive response to the Rio Declaration on Environment and Development in 1992, under the auspices of the State Planning Commission and the State Science and Technology Commission, departments and institutions concerned under the State Council and social organizations prepared "China's Agenda 21st — White Paper on China's Population, Resource Environment and Development in the 21st Century" (for short, "China's Agenda 21st"). This is a strategic plan for sustainable development drawn up according to international standards. With reference to the global "Agenda 21" adopted at the UN Environment and Development Conference in Rio de Janeiro in 1992 and in line with the national conditions in China, it expounds in detail China's views and strategy on sustainable development. The document points out that to strive to seek a road for sustainable development coordinating population, economy, society, environment and resources is necessary for China and the right choice for development in the 21st century. Subsequently, China has issued a series of policies, measures and a plan of action to promote sustainable development.

Sustainable development is a concept covering a wide range of subjects and contents. Here we deal only with population — an important variable affecting sustainable development. We discuss the impacts and challenges it may bring to the country's long-term development, and finally makes an analysis of the correct policy direction concerning the population in order to achieve sustainable development.

(1) Modern Interpretation of the Concept of Development

Since the UN World Commission on Environment and Development issued the report titled "Our Common Future" (also known as "the Bruntland Report") in 1987, the concept of sustainable development has spread like wildfire. The implication of this concept is "development that meets the needs of the present without compromising the ability of future generations to meet their own needs." Sustainable development as an overall, systematic and novel view on de-

131

velopment is of great significance. One, it establishes the relationship between economic growth and sustainable development. That is, the former is the source and condition, and the latter is the objective and destination. Sustained economic growth is the substance and core of sustainable development. The governments of all countries are fully aware of the urgency of reducing and eventually eliminating the pattern of non-sustainable production and consumption, and the importance of making the best use of resources in ways that do not harm the ecology and produce as little waste as possible. Two, the concept of sustainable development has made it clear that the purpose of development is to improve the quality of life of the present and future generations of mankind. An example was the Program of Action adopted at the Cairo Conference in 1994, which pointed out to the effect that the program discussed issues within an overall and comprehensive framework, with a view to improving the quality of life of the present and future generations of the world. Three, the concept of sustainable development stresses that the central issue of sustainable development is social progress and the all-round development of mankind. The Program of Action also points out that the center of the issue of sustainable development is man. Man has the duty to conform with nature, and live a healthy and productive life. The people are the most important and valuable resources of any country. A country should guarantee that all individuals have opportunities to develop their potential. Obviously, this is a modern humanist view of development. Man is the purpose, subject and destination of development. How to provide everyone with equal opportunities to fully develop and tap their potential, and enable the people of both present and future generations to share the fruits of social progress fairly and achieve a pattern for prolonged stability, and civilized and prosperous development. This is indeed a common challenge for the whole of mankind.

What kind of pattern for sustainable development should mankind pursue? From the angle of systematic science, "development" is, in fact, an extremely complicated macro system, which may be seen as the composite state and process of operation of five major subsystems — population, economy, society, environment and resources. In the beginning, sustainable development was a development strategy directed at environmental and resources issues. It was fully reaffirmed at the UN Environment and Development Conference in 1992 as a development objective, pattern and strategy. The Rio Declaration and Agenda 21st abandoned the traditional development pattern, which consumed large quantities of energy and resources at the cost of the quality of the environment. The 1994 Population and Development Conference and the 1995 Social Development Conference gave more prominence to the place and role of the population in the course of sustainable development.

The new approach to development not only puts the all-round development of man in the central position, it also stresses the harmony of the macro system. Comparatively speaking, "harmony" is perhaps even more basic and also more important than "sustainability", as it can better reveal the essential characteristics of a development system. In other words, the first thing is to improve the mutually effecting structural-functional status of the development system, and the second thing is to keep a structural- functional status that promotes the favorable operation of the development system, that is, make it sustainable. Generally speaking, a robustly sustainable system has a high degree of coordination, while a weakly sustainable system naturally has a low degree of coordination. In this sense, only "coordinated development" is true "sustainable development". In other words, if there is not a high degree of coordination as backing among the systems, it will be difficult to continue the sustainable development of any subsystem — such as the sustainable development of the economy or the sustainable development of the environment — and it will be even more difficult to achieve sustainable development in the true sense.

It is important to advance the theory of coordinated development, as it reveals the essential characteristics of a healthy development system. However, it is not easy to judge whether the operation of a development system is coordinated or not, because it involves too many variables. Obviously, a judgment must be made on the "degree of coordination" of the entire development system. There must be a certain critical value threshold (the concept of a "cross-over point") between coordinated development and uncoordinated development. So, by relying on the "critical degree of coordination", we can make a judgment on the value of the structural-functional state of the development system. Here, qualitative inference and quantitative analysis are interdependent. Then, how do we measure the "degree of coordination" of the macro development system? We might as well make the judgment from the results of the operation of the system. As we know, whether it is the development of the population or economic and social development, the ultimate aim of development is the raising of the people's living standards, the improvement of the quality of life and the all-round development of man. Such being the case, we can change the indices for measuring the "degree of coordination" into the criteria for the quality of life and the standards for the quality of the nationals. If the methods of improvement of the quality of life and the national quality are undesirable, and they even become worse, we must find the cause in the process of the actual operation of the development system. To demographers, it is obviously very important to think of the mechanism behind the emergence of population problems in China, and the way to solve them from the angle of "coordinated development".

(2) The Challenge to Sustainable Development

The so-called "difficult population problem" is, of course, more serious than an ordinary population problem. It is often the sudden worsening of the population problem, which shows that the social and economic consequences of the population problem have arisen and may be still worsening. Therefore, the "difficult population problem" is actually a summarization of the phenomenon in which economic development is hindered by population variables and even jeopardizes social stability. It is true that there are different views on the seriousness of the "difficult population problem", but at least the phenomenon show that a difficult population problem really exists in China. The following two major categories of parallel population problems are exactly the overall reflection of the difficult population problem in modern China.

The first is naturally the problem of population growth. The "low fertility rate (or low growth rate) and high increment" has been generalized as a basic characteristic of population growth in China at present and even in the foreseeable future. We have adopted very strict and effective measures to control the population, but because of the large base figure of the population, the population growth in China in the next decades will be unavoidable, and the increase of the population will be an indisputable fact. It is estimated that it will be possible for the Chinese population to reach zero growth around the middle of this century. The growth of the total population will be inevitably accompanied by the pressure of its demands for consumption, education, employment and other services. The food, farmland, education, employment, transport, housing and medical service problems, and many other problems arising from the increased demands can all find the position and role of the population factor in the cause structure.

Moreover, a more realistic and more outstanding structural problem is that of the geographic redistribution of the population, such as the over-urbanization caused by the migration of farmer laborers. In view of the over-concentration of people of rural origin in the cities and new economic growth belts, the Chinese government attaches great importance to this, and has already issued standards for the "orderly and appropriate" migration of rural labor from one region to another. On the surface, the problem of "over-urbanization" seems to be a "population problem", but in essence it is not only a superficial manifestation of the force differential of population pressure, but the reflection of many problems in rural development. It is also a historical product of the uneven social and economic development in the urban and rural areas.

Finally, the problem of the quality of the citizens. The large number of low-quality people will be a latent source of crisis in the course of sustainable social and economic development in the future. It can be expected that with the deepening of the market-oriented economic and social changes, "high-quality human resources" will become an important resource factor in the process of sustainable development, while the advantage of the low price of the low-quality labor will gradually disappear and their obvious skill disadvantage will become conspicuous in the increasingly tight competition. However, it is gratifying to see that the high-quality human resources in China have kept growing. The Chinese government attaches great importance to investment in education, but it will take a long time to improve the quality of the overall population.

It is not difficult for us to find the essence of the "difficult population problem". In the final analysis, it is a problem of social and economic development coupled with the problem of human development. China is now doing its best to find a permanent solution to the difficult population problem through "development". It is essential to attach importance to the three major problems under the present changing conditions: One, the coordinated development of the urban-rural economy and the regional economy; two, human development; and three, the development of human resources. In short, realizing sustainable and coordinated social and economic development, along with human development is the final solution to the difficult problem of the Chinese population.

(3) The Economic Effects of Population Growth: a Dialectical Investigation

The problem of Chinese population growth is an outstanding challenge to sustainable development. In the decades to come, China will remain haunted by the problem of population growth.

The "economic effect of population growth" can be analyzed and appraised from at least two angles: One, by analyzing the effect from the angle of time sequence, it can be divided into short-term and long-term effects; and two, by analyzing it in a sectional way, it can be divided into micro and macro effects. Of course, "population growth" itself is not a simple concept. For example, we can differentiate between the natural growth of the population and the migrating growth of the population, between the relative increment of the population and the absolute increment of the population, between the open growth of the population and the closed growth of the population, between the changing growth of the population and the momentum growth of the population, and between the positive, zero and negative growths of the population. Moreover, the positive and negative growths can each be divided into high- and low-growth categories. When analyzing the effects of population growth, one must differentiate between the growth of the newborn population and the replacement growth of the population in different age groups, either by making a formation analysis of the population born in the same period or making a periodical analysis of the populations in the different formations.

From the short-term or medium-term point of view (ten to twenty years for example), what the growth of the newborn population brings is, first of all, a net consumption effect, but whether from the macro or micro point of view, this relative net consumption effect is not necessarily negative. From the macro point of view, the newborn population as a consumption force is manifested as a net denominator effect. That is, if the gross production remains the same, the per-capita amount possessed is bound to fall. Consumption also promotes production. Production and consumption are not separate, but have a kind of interdependent cyclic relationship. The newborn population increases the size of the consumption demand, and thereby enriches the demand structure. This is an important population push — in a healthy structure in which the social economy can operate well and the production mechanism can give sensitive feedback to the market. This population push undoubtedly promotes the development of the productive forces. In other words, the denominator effect of the population is not simply manifested as the existence of a consumer force. It also induces the expansion of the productive forces.[62] Therefore, if we look at the denominator effect of the population from the angle of linking production with consumption, we very easily find the "bridge" between the denominator effect of the population (in a sense, this can be regarded as an embodiment of the consumption function of the population) and the numerator effect of the population (in a sense, this can be regarded as an embodiment of the production function of the population). From the short-term point of view, it is clear that, as far as the consumption effect of family population growth is concerned, when the disposable income remains relatively unchanged, the growth of the family population will result in a fall in the per-capita possession of means of subsistence and consumption, thus affecting the living standards of the family for a given period of time. However, whether from the macro or micro point of view, the rational boundary for population growth should be defined not from a short-term, but from a long-term perspective.

The long-term economic effect of population growth is an integrated effect, consisting of both the consumption effect and the production effect. From the angle of the need for subsistence, the population as a consumption force should be unconditional. However, the population also has the aspect of a productive force. Social and economic development is inseparable from the development of human resources. Labor is the most active factor of the productive forces, and the quality of labor in particular is playing an increasingly important role in the modern economy. At present, the active labor force is also realizing the replacement growth of the population.

Without population growth, there is no way of training a new generation of workers, and economic vigor will inevitably decline. This is one of the long-term consequences of the present low fertility, and a current headache for the developed industrialized countries hit by a shortage of labor. Moreover, from the quantitative point of view, what we need is an appropriate growth of the population. The population growth rate in China has fallen to a fairly low level. This is a historical legacy, caused by an excessively large base figure and markedly young age structure — a product of the momentum of growth. From the regional angle, the growth of the urban population through migration may also become a source of the replacement growth of the working population. From the micro angle, once a member of a family grows up to become a member of the employed population, this inevitably increases the income elasticity of the micro population growth, thus making it possible for a family to improve its living standard.

It can thus be seen that the economic effect of population growth is complicated, and one cannot make a simple appraisal of it. From the long-term point of view, population growth also has a positive effect that cannot be ignored. Julian L. Simon, a U.S. economist, expounded this in detail in his book *The Economics of Population Growth*. His main conclusion based on the situation in developing countries is that from the long-term point of view moderate population growth has a much better economic effect than zero or excessive growth.[63] The accepted wisdom in China is that, in a condition of overpopulation, a new round of population growth inevitably leads to an increase in pressure from the consumption and other demands (especially employment). However, the situation is not so simple if the effect of population growth can be appraised in conjunction with social and economic development against the background of reform and opening. Overpopulation in whatever sense — over-subsistence and over-employment are inseparable from the criteria of social and economic development under given historical conditions. The former can be regarded as an "environmental optimum population", and the latter as an "economic optimum population". The concrete standards may differ from time to time, depending on the standards for the quality of life and the goal of social development. Of course, if social and economic development is relative in a given time, the population growth in the same period may make the problem of overpopulation even more serious. In fact, however, in the long and medium term, it is difficult to grasp the variables of social and economic development. Therefore, it is a simplification to say that population growth inevitably leads to aggravation of the problem of overpopulation.

The conclusion is that the increment of the Chinese population is astonishing and irreversible, but its economic effect is not completely negative. In view of this, it is better to take population growth into consideration in the course of long-term social and economic development, and seek a relatively objective and fair answer based on multiple value standards.

(4) Analysis of the Population Policy for Achieving Sustainable Development

When we pursue the goal of sustainable development, what population conditions should we prepare and what population environment should we create? Population as a special "resource" and sustainable development promote and restrain each other. The variability of the population is one of the basic factors for realizing sustainable development. In other words, optimizing the population conditions and environment is the basic social condition for the realization of sustainable development.

In discussions on sustainable development, people usually show concern for the relations between the environment and development, but what genuine sustainable development involves is not only the problem of the permanent use of resources and the problem of ecological balance, but also the problem of whether development of the population is rational, appropriate and healthy. Therefore, when we design a strategy for population development within the framework of sustainable development, an important matter is to regard population as a long-term variable and to consider the problem of the development of the population instead of the problem of the growth of the population over a fairly long period of time; in other words, the problem is one of paying overall attention to the quantity, quality and structure of the population.

Theoretically, it is not difficult to define the population conditions and environment suitable for sustainable development, namely, appropriate size, good quality of the nationals and a rational population structure. However, so far as the concrete national conditions in China are concerned, the available population conditions and environment are not good. In order to improve the existing population conditions and environment determined by history, it is essential to take pains to control the quantity of the population, improve the quality of the population and optimize the population structure. In concrete terms, the government attaches great importance to improving the quality of the citizens and implanting the "idea of sustainable development" in their minds. The optimization of the population structure not only refers to keeping the balance in the sociological sense in the evolution of the sex and age structure of the population, but also to the rational distribution of the population in terms of space, and at the same time the optimization of the employment structure of the working population. Relatively speaking, the significance of controlling the quantity of the population to the level of "sustainable development" is indirect and extended. In any case, the realization of the goal of a low fertility rate is of great importance to a country with a serious overpopulation problem it has alleviated the pressure of the population growth that would have been even greater, and reduced the increment of the population, thus winning more precious time and room for sustainable coordinated development. However, the realization of a low fertility rate does not mean that the problem of population growth has disappeared, and of course, even less the end of the population problem. In fact, the rapid fall of the fertility rate is helpful for development, but has not fundamentally removed the population obstacle to sustainable development. As we know, the purpose of controlling the population is to strive to create the best possible population conditions and environment for sustainable development. But population control and the following slowdown of the population growth rate will not necessarily help to achieve sustainable development.

As stated above, sustainable development should center on the all-round development of man, which is the central issue as well as the ultimate objective. The prerequisite for the development of man is the improvement of the quality of the population. Therefore, theoretically, we can fully assert that the problem of the quality of the population is the key problem arising in the course of pursuing sustainable development. In this regard, China has paid great attention to the "quality of the citizens", the population condition that most needs optimization and the goal that most needs to be attained. To coordinate the relations between the population and sustainable development, an important consideration on the part of the government is to strive to improve the overall quality of the citizens, and especially to implant the "idea of sustainable development" deeply in their minds, thereby making society conscious of avoiding all short-sighted actions.

The quality of the population is no more than a synonym for the amalgamation of competitiveness, productive force and coordinating force. Today, when the reform and opening policies are accelerating in depth, we must keep in mind that the quality of the people is the one thing that cannot be imported. The essence of rejuvenating the country through science and technology is "building the country by relying on the quality of the people." The prosperity of a country needs people of outstanding talent, but does not rely on such people alone. Fundamentally speaking, it relies on the improvement of the average quality of the whole people and the display of their enthusiasm and creative power. All countries which have been able to achieve sustained economic growth and sustainable development have attached importance to the improvement of the quality of their citizens, and workers in particular. To be brief, the development of man is the most important development.

Reference Documents

[1] *A History of Views on China's Population*, by Wu Shenyuan, published by China Social Sciences Press, Beijing, 1986

[2] *Population: China's Sword of Damocles*, by He Qinlian, published by Sichuan People's Publishing House, Chengdu

[3] *Complete Works of Marx and Engels* (Vol. 7)

[4] *Forum on Chinese Population Growth and Food Supply in the 21st Century* (One and Two), *Analysis of the Market and the Population*, 1996 (3~4), *Forum on Population and Development* (11), "Population Growth and the Food Problem in China", *Population Studies*, 1993 (3)

[5] "Inquiry into and Analysis of the Law of the Proportional Development of the Population", by Mu Guangzong, *Population Studies*, 1989 (1) and "Population Operation Mechanism: A Historical Study", by Mu Guangzong, *Population Monthly*, 1989 (5)

[6] *Ditto*, (2)

[7] "The Development of the Chinese Population and the Peasant Uprisings in the 18th and 19th Centuries", by Liu Lei, *Monthly Journal of Sichuan Teachers University*, 1988 (4)

[8] *Ditto*, [2]

[9] *The Small-scale Peasant Economy and Social Vicissitudes in North China*, by Huang Zongzhi (USA), Zhong Hua Book Company, Beijing, 1986

[10] *A Study of Per-mu Yields of Food Grains in Chinese History*, by Wu Hui, Agricultural Publishing House, Beijing, 1985

[11] *Ditto*, [9]

[12] *Ditto*, [2]

[13] *The United States and China*, by John King Fairbanks (USA), The Commercial Press, Beijing, 1973

[14] *Ditto*, [1]

[15] *Ditto*, [9]

[16] "On Labor and Wages", by Ma Wenrui, *Xinhua Fortnightly*, 1956 (15)

[17] *Two Theories of Production and the Chinese Population Problem*, by Liao Tianping, Guangdong People's Publishing House, Guangzhou, 1982

[18] *Selected Works of Zhou Enlai* (Vol. II), People's Publishing House, Beijing, 1984

[19] *Documents and Studies* (1983), People's Publishing House, 1984

[20] "On the Question of Correctly Handling the Contradictions among the People", by Mao Zedong, *Selected Works of Mao Zedong* (5), People's Publishing House, Beijing, 1977

[21] "The Relations Between the Population Issue and the Development of the Productive Forces in China", by Ma

Yinchu, *Collection of Economic Theses* (Vol. II), Beijing University Press, Beijing, 1981

[22] *New Population Theory*, by Ma Yinchu, Beijing Press, Beijing, 1979

[23] *Chinese Yearbook of Statistics*, China Economic Press, Beijing, 1983

[24] *The Road of Change to Modern Population — Experience and Theory on the Southern Jiangsu Model*, by Wu Cangping, China Science and Technology Press, 1993

[25] United States, *World Population Monitor*, 1983

[26] "Changes in the Fertility Rate and the Aging of the Population in China", by Chen Wei, *Population Studies*, 1993

[27] "Seeing the Problem of the Chinese Population in a New Light", by Gu Baochang and Mu Guangzong, *Population Studies*, 1994

[28] *Economic Development in the Third World* (Vol. I), by M.P. Todaro (USA), Chinese People's University Press, 1988

[29] *Study of Population Countermeasures to Eliminate Poverty*, by Zhang Chunyuan, China Higher Education Press, 1996

[30] "Low Fertility Rate, the Market Economy and China's Population Control", by Wu Cangping and Mu Guangzong, *China Population Science*, 1996 (3)

[31] Challenge and Growth: Theoretical Basis for Population Control, by Mu Guangzong and Hou Dongmin, *Population Monthly*, 1993 (3)

[32] "The Problem of Population and Development in China — Address at the 18th Pacific Science Conference", by Peng Peiyun, *China Population Journal*, June 16, 1995

[33] "The New Population Issue in the Course of the First Fall of the Chinese Fertility Rate and a Roundup of the Symposium on its Solution", by Mu Guangzong and Chen Wei, *Population Studies*, 1994 (5)

[34] "Theoretical Explanations for the Rapid Fall in the Chinese Fertility Rate", by Wu Cangping, *Population Studies*, 1986 (1)

[35] *The People's Daily*, March 21, 1994

[36] "Outline of Studies on the Fall in the Chinese Fertility Rate and Its Consequences", by Mu Guangzong; "My Understanding of Population Aging and the Aged Population Problem in the Course of the Fall in the Chinese Fertility Rate", by Qiao Xiaochun; "A Study of the Consequences of the Fall in the Chinese Fertility Rate and the Macro Economy", by Zhang Zhigang; "A Study of the Fall in the Chinese Fertility Rate and its Consequences: The Individual Case of Shanghai", by Zhu Guohong, 1994

[37] "Address at the Second Executive Council Meeting of the China Population Welfare Fund", by Peng Peiyun, 1994

[38] "Family Planning and Guarantee of Human Rights, by Cha Ruichuan", *Population Studies*, 1993 (5)

[39] "Seeing the Chinese Population Issue in a New Light", by Gu Baochang and Mu Guangzong, *Population Studies*, 1994 (5)

[40] "Changes in the Chinese Fertility Rate and the Ag-

ing of the Population", by Chen Wei, *Population Studies*, 1993 (5)

[41] "The Induced Change of the Fertility Rate — On the Effectiveness of Chinese Population Planning and Social and Economic Changes", Tian Xinyuan (USA), *Science and Technology Review*, 1986 (1); "Theoretical Explanations for the Rapid Fall in the Chinese Fertility Rate", Wu Cangping, *Population Studies*, 1986 (1); "On the Spontaneous and Induced Changes of the Population", Song Ruilai, *China Population Science*, 1991 (2)

[42] "The Social and Economic Consequences of the Changes in the Fertility Rate", by Zhu Guohong, *Social Science Front*, 1992 (1)

[43] "The Aging of the Population and the Natural Negative Elimination of the Population", by Mu Guangzong, *China Social Science Quarterly*, 1995 (Autumn)

[44] "The Advantages and Disadvantages of the Chinese Population from the Angle of the Resources", by Mu Guangzong, *Population and Economy*, 1994 (2)

[45] "The Guiding Principles and Measures of the Central Labor and Employment Commission Concerning the Solution to the Rural Surplus Labor Problem" (Oct. 31, 1952); "State Council Directive on the Prevention of Unplanned Rural Population Movements" (Dec. 30, 1956), *China Population Yearbook*, 1985

[46] *China Without Balance* (Part I), by Guo Shutian and Liu Chunbin, Hebei People's Publishing House, Shijiazhuang, 1991

[47] *A Theory of Migration*, by Everett S. Lee, edited by

J.A. Jackson, Cambridge University Press, 1969 (282~297)

The Field of Vision of Social Demography — Translations of Selected Social Demographic Theses in the West, by Gu Baochang, Commercial Press, Beijing, 1992

[48] "An Attempt of Strategic Significance — Report on the Establishment of the System for the Transfer of Land-use Rights in Luliang Prefecture, Shanxi Province" (I and II), *Guangming Daily*, April 10, 1994

[49] "Guest Peasants Contract Farmland Away from Home", *Xinhua Daily*, June 17, 1994

[50] *The Population Problem*, by Chen Da, Commercial Press, 1934

[51] *New Population Theory*, by Ma Yinchu, Beijing Press, Beijing, 1979

[52] *A Course in Population Theories*, by Liu Zheng, Chinese People's University Press, Beijing, 1985

[53] "A New Theory of the Quality of the Population", by Mu Guangzong, *Population Studies*, 1989 (3)

[54] "Modernization and the Quality of the Population", by Zhu Guohong, *Population Studies*, 1990 (5)

"The Quality of the Population and Economic Development", by Xu Jinsheng, *Population Studies*, 1991 (4)

[55] "On the Negative Elimination of the Quality of the Population", by Zhou Xiaozheng, *Sociological Studies*, 1991 (3)

[56] "On the Quality Control of the Chinese Population", by Mu Guangzong, *Sociological Studies*, 1991 (3)

[57] "Towards the 21st Century: The Regional Differences in the Development of the Chinese Population", by Li Fude and Liu Jintang, *Population Studies*, 1996 (2)

[58] "Analysis of the Prospects for the Development of the Chinese Population", by Zhang Lingguang and Jiang Zhenghua, *Chinese Population Science*, 1995 (3)

[59] "A Roundup of the Symposium on the New Population Problems in the Course of the Second Fall in the Chinese Fertility Rate, and Solutions", by Mu Guangzong and Chen Wei, *Population Studies*, 1995 (5)

[60] "Some Problems in the Course of the Development of the Future Population in China", by Zeng Yi and Jin Wobai (USA), *China Social Sciences*, 1991 (3)

[61] *A Study of the Course of the Aging of the Chinese Population*, by Du Peng, Chinese People's University Press, 1994 and 1996

[62] "'Large Population' Is not the Synonym for 'Population Burden'", by Wen Long, *Population Studies*, 1996

[63] *Population Growth Economics*, by Julian L. Simon (USA), translated by Peng Songjian, *et al.*, Beijing University Press, Beijing, 1984

About the Authors

Wu Cangping, born in Panyu, Guangdong Province, in 1922, is a professor at the Population Research Institute of the Chinese People's University and a supervisor of Ph.D candidates. He graduated from the Department of Economics of Lingnan University in 1946, and completed his studies at the Business School of New York University in 1950 with an MBA degree. He is now a member of the National Committee of the Chinese People's Political Consultative Conference, deputy head of the Population Group of the CPPCC National Committee, president of the China Society of Gerontology, vice chairman of the China Population Society, honorary president of the Beijing Population Society, council member of the International Society of Gerontology and council member of the Cooperation Committee of the International Population Studies Institutes. He has written, translated or taken part in the writing and translation of some 30 works, and has had more than 200 papers published. He has won a dozen prizes for his writings and papers at the ministerial, provincial and municipal levels. In 1996, he won the Second Zhonghua (China) Award (Science Award) and a first prize for human studies and social sciences from the State Education Commission. Among his leading works are *The World Population*, *Population Statistics* and *A Survey of Population*.

Mu Guangzong, born in 1964 in Ningbo, Zhejiang Province, is an associate professor with the Population Research

Institute of the Chinese People's University. He is now head of the Population Theory Teaching and Research Section of the Demography Department, and a Ph.D. candidate. He is also a member of the Population and Economy Commission of the China Demographic Society and a member of the China Society of Gerontology. He has had more than 200 papers and books published and has won many prizes for excellent papers and achievements in scientific research at the ministerial and national levels. In 1994, he won one of the First Outstanding Social Sciences Achievement Awards for Young People. Among his most outstanding works are *The "Population Bucket Theory" and Economic Development*, *A Study of Low Fertility*, *To Whom Will China's Future Be Bequeathed — An Urgent Report on the Only-child Problems* and *The Dual Economy and China's Population Control*.

图书在版编目（CIP）数据

中国人口的现状与对策/邬沧萍，穆光宗 著.
一北京：外文出版社，2003.9
（聚焦中国丛书）
ISBN 7-119-03326-3
Ⅰ.中… Ⅱ.①邬…②穆… Ⅲ.人口－研究－中国－英文
Ⅳ. C924.24
中国版本图书馆 CIP 数据核字（2003）第 031597 号

英文翻译	章挺权	英文改稿	Paul White
英文审定	黄友义	责任编辑	蔡莉莉
装帧设计	蔡 荣	印刷监制	张国祥

中国人口的现状与对策

邬沧萍 穆光宗 著

*

©外文出版社
外文出版社出版
（中国北京百万庄大街 24 号）
邮政编码　100037
外文出版社网址 http://www.flp.com.cn
外文出版社电子信箱: info@flp.com.cn
sales@flp.com.cn
三河汇鑫印务有限公司印刷
中国国际图书贸易总公司发行
（中国北京车公庄西路 35 号）
北京邮政信箱第 399 号　邮政编码　100044
2004 年(小 16 开)第 1 版
2004 年 4 月第 1 版第 1 次印刷
（英）
ISBN 7-119-03326-3/Z・640(外)
02300(平)
17-E-3546 P